DANC in the DESERT

*Spiritual Refreshment
for Your Parched Soul*

Marsha Crockett

InterVarsity Press
Downers Grove, Illinois

InterVarsity Press
P.O. Box 1400, Downers Grove, IL 60515-1426
World Wide Web: www.ivpress.com
E-mail: mail@ivpress.com

InterVarsity Press® is the book-publishing division of InterVarsity Christian Fellowship/USA®, a student movement active on campus at hundreds of universities, colleges and schools of nursing in the United States of America, and a member movement of the International Fellowship of Evangelical Students. For information about local and regional activities, write Public Relations Dept., InterVarsity Christian Fellowship/USA, 6400 Schroeder Rd., P.O. Box 7895, Madison, WI 53707-7895, or visit the IVCF website at <www.ivcf.org>.

Cover design: Cindy Kiple

Cover image: lady dancing: Eastcott Momatiuk/Getty Images
          desert: Barbara Leslie/Getty Images

ISBN 0-8308-2384-0

Printed in the United States of America ∞

Library of Congress Cataloging-In-Publication Data

Crockett, Marsha, 1957-

  Dancing in the desert: spiritual refreshment for your parched soul/
by Marsha Crockett
    p. cm.
Includes bibliographical references.
   ISBN 0-8308-2384-0 (pbk.: alk. paper)
   1. Consolation. 2. Spiritual life—Christianity. I. Title.
  BV4905.3 .C76 2003
  248.8'6—dc 21

                                       2002152083

P	19	18	17	16	15	14	13	12	11	10	9	8	7	6	5	4	3	2	1
Y	19	18	17	16	15	14	13	12	11	10	09	08	07	06	05	04	03		

Dedicated to Timm and Karen Jackson,

Dearest friends and colaborers in Christ.

Your endless love and encouragement, offered in Jesus' name,

have been my stream in the desert.

CONTENTS

ACKNOWLEDGMENTS

Many have touched my life and faithfully ministered to me as I worked my way through this project. But I would be remiss without recognizing the consistent and large contribution of these faithful ones:

My Tuesday morning writers group—Linda, Betty, Judy, Jane, Marion, Donna, Sharon and several others who have helped along the way—after four years together, I'm still excited about how God works in the midst of such a diverse group of women. Your friendship, as well as your professional input, is my great treasure.

My church family at Canyon Creek Community Church and, in particular, my "Early Riser" group—year after year you teach me what it means to be one in Christ. You've been his hands and feet, his voice and ears. May he bless you in ever-increasing measure as he has so richly blessed me through you.

My family far and near—parents, siblings, aunts, uncles, cousins—you have given me more joy than any one person should have a right to enjoy.

My sweet daughters, Megan and Amy—thanks for sharing computer time with me and for hanging in there through the ups and downs of life. I love you dearly, and I'm so proud of who you are, knowing that God is faithfully completing the work he has begun in your lives.

Finally, my editor and friend, Cindy Bunch, and the staff at InterVarsity Press—your dedication and excellence shine with the true quality of "working as unto the Lord." I'm honored to partner with you to accomplish all that Christ has equipped us to do together.

INTRODUCTION

I've been a desert dweller most of my life. Living in Arizona, I know how to endure the heat. I know not to go outdoors without my SPF lotion. I know how to drive in a blinding dust storm and how to climb a mountain. I know which plants survive the hellish heat of summer and how to prepare rock-hard soil for seedlings to thrive. But none of my practical knowledge prepared me to face the spiritual desert where I lived for over a year.

I can't say that any one event triggered my desert journey, though several may have contributed. I seemed to have arrived there gradually, moving from a lush mountaintop forest of spiritual delight down into desert-dry grasses interspersed with the pines. An occasional cactus appeared among the trees, but I ignored its spiny intrusion. Finally I discovered myself surrounded by thorny, scrubby vegetation and hard, dry dirt, and suddenly I wondered, *When did I arrive in the desert?* Change is the one constant in this life, but sometimes even the subtle changes drop us unexpectedly into arid conditions where we thirst for God's presence in a new way.

What's it like to live in a spiritual desert? Such experiences are unique to each sojourner. For me, some days I drank water from the rocks, unaware that my refreshment came from the hand of God. Other days I felt buried by the sand and wondered if I would ever see the light, if I would ever feel the breath of God reviving my soul. I often traveled at night, through the darkness, but I always pressed toward hope—hope for a brighter path and a more hospitable climate. Despite the stark conditions, there is a sense of freedom there as one strips away all the unnecessary baggage of trivial living and takes only what is needed to survive.

Everyone who walks with God eventually arrives at the outer edge of a spiritual desert. What puts us into these places? Life—disappointment, weariness, crisis, discontentment, selfishness, confusion, death, darkness and waiting. Any one or all of these circumstances can send us packing into the wilderness where God tests our faith. But often the reason why we arrive in the desert remains a mystery. We may feel abandoned, fidgety and restless as God's all-consuming silence descends on us in the heat of the day.

It is easy to make fatal mistakes on a desert journey. When we're thirsty, we begin the hunt for water. We scan the horizon, peering through waves of heat rising from the parched ground. We survey the mountains, the scrub brush, the rocks and cacti. Perhaps a low spot just over the rise has collected a puddle of water. And so we expend our energy moving from one low spot to the next in the heat of the day, believing that eventually we will come upon a watering hole. If only we understood that the water lies hidden in the mountain rocks above.

Soon our every thought pivots on the vision of water. We will do anything to find it and to leave the barren land behind. But to survive in the desert requires that we move more slowly and travel more deeply into it. It asks that we go farther than what humanly makes sense. It is ironic that in the desert we come to know water so intimately. "If you want to study water, you do not go to the Amazon or to Seattle. You come here, to the driest land. Nowhere else is it drawn to such a point. In the desert, water is unedited, perfect."[1]

So it is as we enter into a spiritual desert journey. We may search desperately for relief, but God calls us to thirst for him more. We may long for his refreshment, but we will never enjoy it until we have lived without it. For in the desert, the life-giving Living Water awaits us in its purest, most soul-quenching form. If we are willing to relinquish our own plans and pursue the voice that calls us to climb higher, we will find that the spiritual desert is not a God-forsaken land, although we may be blinded to his presence and provision. We fight against its harsh reality as we struggle to find our way out. We consider what we can do to reach a more hospitable climate. We pray harder, confess more sin and do more good deeds, but usually to no avail. And all the while we miss the joy of his hidden presence.

So where does the dancing come in? Is it possible to enjoy this experience, to not only survive but to actually thrive? The desert is not a welcoming place at first glance. But eventually we learn that "the desert . . . is not a problem to be solved but a mysterious place to dwell for a while."[2] As God told Isaac in the midst of a famine, so he says to us: "Stay in this land for a while and I will be with you and will bless you" (Genesis 26:2-3). And so we turn to God. At first, in fits of frustration, we shake a fist at him and fling our complaints against him. "Why, God? Why are you so far away?" Finally we realize that all we can do is be silent and move when the cloud of his presence guides or stop when the fire of his glory flames in the night sky.

When God leads us to the desert, he goes with us, stays near us and speaks to us in spaces of deep quietness. As the psalmist wrote, "Deep calls to deep," and from our deep, silent longings for God, deep trust, hope, love and joy gush from a dry land. In this otherworldly place, we rest our head on rock pillows, we sweeten our drink with wooden sticks, and we watch bread rain down from heaven's oven to satisfy our deepest hunger.

The pages of this book flow from the wilderness regions of my own spiritual walk with God. Desert travel requires a slowed pace, and I've allowed time for you to walk slowly and explore your soul thirst too. You'll even find "Rest Stops" along the way, and I encourage you to use a journal to reflect on your journey (see appendix). Picture these pauses as a cool, quiet place where God shelters you in the cleft of the rock—a place to regroup and meet with him in your desert. Eventually you'll come to the "Rivers of Delight" where God encourages you to dwell with him as he prepares this time and place just for you. You'll also share a "Desert Journey" through the eyes of biblical characters who walked through a spiritual wilderness. At the end of each chapter, you'll find a section entitled "Hidden Joy." Use this for a more in-depth personal study or as discussion questions for a small group setting.

Each chapter is designed for an extended time with God. However, you can enjoy short segments of time as you study through a chapter over several days. Or set aside an hour or two to be alone with the Lord. Whether it is a few minutes throughout the week or a concentrated time with God, don't feel rushed to leave the desert, to finish the chapter or even finish the book. Receive these words and this time as a gift from

God to revive your spirit and rebuild your heart.

I pray that my words and, above all, the Word of Life will refresh you and help you realize that you are not alone in the desert. Some have journeyed ahead of you, others will follow behind, but always God walks with you and dwells in you as you learn to live in the shelter of his wings. And when he meets you in the heat of the day and whispers his love into the wilderness of your heart, then you will discover hidden joy, and you will want to give a shout, shake a tambourine and join in the desert dance.

1

CONTENTMENT . . .

in the Desert of Desire

> *It is just, O Lord, that those who are not satisfied with the divine bounty of the present moment, which pours down on them from the Father of Light, should be punished by being unable to find contentment in anything.*
>
> JEAN-PIERRE DE CAUSSADE,
> *SACRAMENT OF THE PRESENT MOMENT*

QUIET YOUR HEART

Read Psalm 86:10-13. Make the phrase "Give me an undivided heart" your prayer today. Picture your heart and your life fragmented by the demands, desires, sins, disappointments and distractions of the day. Then picture God tenderly picking up the pieces and putting them together. All your longings, all those fragments, now rest in his hands, and your heart beats as one with his. He has given you an "undivided heart."

ENTER HIS PRESENCE

Read 1 Chronicles 29:11-13, and meditate on God's all-encompassing, all-sufficient character as you begin to contemplate your thirst for contentment in him. After you have come before him with a quiet heart, ask him to open your ears to his voice on your journey toward contentment.

I SIT AT MY DESK IN THE MIDST OF THE TECHNOLOGY that literally wraps itself around me, and stare at the computer screen for I don't know how long—long enough to sense a discontentment buried deep inside me. Without words, I ask God, "What is it?" I shift my eyes to the slender statuette of a faceless woman standing tall and straight, draped in deep purple from head to toe, her head slightly bowed. In her hands she cradles a basket holding three white blossoms—peace lilies.

This figurine symbolizes for me the act of prayer, not the kind of prayer that brings a basket full of concerns, requests and an agenda to God but rather the kind of prayer I pray on days like today when I simply come to God empty, thirsty for his touch, his voice, his presence. Most days my basket brims with tight schedules for family, work and ministry. At times the high-pitched hum of activity masks a low moan of discontentment deep inside. But on quiet days I hear that distant cry that drives me to wish away my life, hoping I will find happiness waiting just around the corner.

The more aware I become of this feeling, the more I know God wants me to pay attention to it. So I begin to face it head on with as much honesty as I can muster and as much openness to God as I can risk. And he gives me insight into my outward dilemma: When I was single, I wanted a meaningful career. After I entered the work force, I wanted to be married. After I was married, I was sure satisfaction would come with children. After children, I wanted to quit my job and stay home. After I was home with the kids, I felt isolated and wanted to go back to work. On and on, I continued looking forward and checking back, longing for purpose and satisfaction. If only I had known it was so close at hand.

But I fail to look beneath my own two feet and see the ground where I stand as a holy place to meet God. I feel trapped in a barren desert of past regrets and future wishes. I constantly try to change my outer circumstances, hoping to find inner contentment, only to be disappointed again and again.

I also become aware of how much the thirst for contentment permeates every aspect of our culture. It is so ingrained in the way we do life that we are blind to its enticements and deaf to its false claims to satisfy our souls. We don't intend to chase after discontentment as we grab for all we can get and sample all that is offered. We pack our shopping carts, our calendars and our minds with fading fun or the tyranny of the urgent. We may not be naive enough to believe we will find deep meaning and purpose in such pursuits, but perhaps we hope to at least make our days bearable.

We teach our children that they must try every sport at least once, and we sign them up for as many personal interest classes as our bank accounts and palm pilots allow. In doing so, we falsely assume that we elevate their sense of self-worth. But what we may be teaching them is that they can never be truly happy and fulfilled without grasping every opportunity presented by the world. What great practice for learning to cover the reality of living with the speed of doing.

God created us with a need to be fed and filled, yet our desires seemingly go unmet. In striving to find fulfillment, our longings may swing wildly out of balance into realms of addiction. Left unchecked, our misplaced contentment crashes into our empty lives as we attempt to fill up on "treasures" that devastate not only our pocketbooks but also our souls.

GAINING PERSPECTIVE

When I look this reality in the face, I realize that my spirit is as void as the surface of the deep before God created the world. One more demand or disappointment can fling me into the outer limits of my ability to cope, and that's when I realize I have pushed myself so hard that I am stumbling along in my walk with God as my legs hurry ahead of my heart. I've joined the throng of others living wrung-out, over-committed, techno-weary lives, grabbing for a little peace and a whole lot of comfort but always pulling up short of my yearning for deep inner contentment.

Author and teacher Tricia McCary Rhodes explains, "We are created to want more, to desire something glorious and grand, and no amount of denying this will change it. The problem is we settle for the limited pleasures of this world, demonstrating that our desires are, as C. S. Lewis wrote, 'not too strong, but too weak.'"[1] In our pursuit for contentment, we fail to pause and simply be content in the glory of God. These outward signs of discontentment reveal inner obstacles to true contentment.

Looking back. When our hearts look back as time moves us

forward, it blinds us to the joys of the present moment or the challenges for growth found in today. In the book of Genesis we read the story of Lot's wife. As she left the sin and decimation of Sodom and Gomorrah and approached the safety of God's grace, the pull of the past caused her to look back, to verify that what lay before her was better than what she left behind. As a result, she lost it all (Genesis 19:15-29). So often we live with regrets and deep wonder about the past. We look over our shoulders, checking and rechecking to see if things have changed. Our past failures or heartaches can lead us into a stream of negative talk that seeps into the language of today's joys: *I can't, I should have, if only, I wish I would have.* Such phrases put the brakes on any potential for change, growth or contentment in God.

Looking forward. Maybe we have dealt with our past heartaches and failures. Maybe it is the future that keeps us from resting contentedly in God's provision. We begin to worry and fret over what may happen. Our thoughts begin, *What if?* as we walk down the path of life like Dorothy on her way to Oz. Fears of what may be chant through our minds like "lions and tigers and bears." Only our song may sound like "failure, rejection and loss, oh my." On the other hand, the future can tempt us to bury ourselves beneath dreams of "somewhere over the rainbow," as we excavate tomorrow's hopes and perceived rewards and dump them on the joy of today. We dig deep into the bottomless pockets of tomorrow, searching for something to make today worthwhile.

Looking in the mirror. And finally, if we are able to shake free from the grip of the past and the enticement of the future, we may yet stumble as we look at ourselves in the mirror of today.

In writing about the life of Jean-Pierre de Caussade, Richard Foster notes, "Once we can face, before God, who we truly are, we have stepped onto the path of grace that leads to conformity to the image of Christ. But the courage to face the inner monsters takes a faith and trust in God that many of us do not possess (or don't want to possess), and so we busy ourselves with muchness and manyness and undertake our colossal enterprises to avoid looking inside."[2] What a shame to refuse to embrace the emptiness, the darkness, and the dryness and thus miss the first stepping stone to knowing God and being filled by his love.

Whether it is our past accomplishments or hurts, our future desires or fears, or the sight of who we truly are, these personal obstacles may keep contentment at bay as we allow them to lord themselves over us. God warns us that seeking our own brand of contentment apart from him is futile, for

> the bed is too short to stretch out on,
> the blanket too narrow to wrap around you. (Isaiah 28:20)

REST STOP

How do you view each of these personal obstacles in your own life? Describe how that obstacle may negatively impact your present happiness. Are there other obstacles God may want you to consider?

RIVERS OF DELIGHT

Before we fully discredit and disarm discontentment, let's look at it in another light. Sometimes discontentment is a good sign. It acknowledges our incompleteness, our yearning for fulfillment in the emptiness of our souls. The psalmist expressed this longing over and over again:

> Oh God, you are my God,
>   earnestly I seek you;
> my soul thirsts for you,
>   my body longs for you,
> in a dry and weary land
>   where there is no water. (Psalm 63:1)

And again in Psalm 42:1:

> As the deer pants for streams of water,
>   so my soul pants for you, O God.

True contentment begins as a holy discontentment, a longing planted in our hearts by God himself: "I will give them a heart to know me, that I am the LORD" (Jeremiah 24:7). Perhaps the best way to understand God's complete ability to satisfy our souls lies in his unrelenting desire to reveal himself to us, hoping that we will accept his invitation to know him in new and intimate ways when we worship his name and his character. He gives us these truths—glimpses of his glory—to satisfy our thirsty souls.

There is no other. God makes it clear in Scripture that he alone invites us to unharness ourselves from the world and breathe a sigh of relief.

> For this is what the LORD says—
> he who created the heavens,
>   he is God;
> he who fashioned and made the earth,
>   he founded it;
> he did not create it to be empty,
>   but formed it to be inhabited—

he says:
"I am the LORD,
    and there is no other.
I have not spoken in secret,
    from somewhere in a land of darkness;
I have not said to Jacob's descendants,
    'Seek me in vain.'
I, the LORD, speak the truth;
    I declare what is right . . .
for I am God, and there is no other." (Isaiah 45:18-19, 22)

Like the earth from which we were formed, God didn't create us for emptiness but rather to be filled by his Spirit. We are his temple, and only when we allow the Holy One into his rightful place does contentment reign. There is no other path to contentment but straight through our Creator, the only one willing to peaceably inhabit our hearts.

He is the Prince of Peace. Searching for contentment in the pleasures of this world continuously stirs up our souls as we remain on a relentless hunt for satisfaction. In contrast, when we turn to our Maker, the One who set the longings of our heart in motion, peace reigns. Vain searching and striving cease. He says simply, "Be still, and know that I am God" (Psalm 46:10). The effect of his presence is "quietness and confidence forever"; we will live "in peaceful dwelling places . . . in undisturbed places of rest" (Isaiah 32:18). What a message for this hurry-up, soul-weary world.

He dwells with us. The name given to our Savior and recorded by Isaiah is Emmanuel, which means "God with us." God's presence isn't an on-again, off-again relationship based on whether he feels like being near us. Nor is it based on how hard we beg him to come. Compare the reality of his nearness to the false comforts of this world that stand afar off where we can't examine too closely their deceitful claims of comfort.

But God came near to us through his Son. He revealed himself as a baby, a form that cries to be picked up, held close, examined and loved. God walks with us every day, regardless of our circumstances or our moods or our ability to sense his nearness. When we don't have the strength to pray, he does it for us. When we are so broken by sin that all we can do is lie in pieces at his feet, he picks us up and heals our hearts.

His message from beginning to end is "I am with you." In the Garden of Eden, God walked with Adam and Eve. In the closing book of Revelation, we read, "Here I am! I stand at the door and knock. If anyone hears my voice and opens the door, I will come in to him and eat with him, and he with me" (Revelation 3:20). How humbling to follow not only the Almighty God of all creation but also the God who comes very near to dwell within our hearts.

REST STOP

Which picture of God do you most long to know and why? Tell God of your longing for him to dwell with you and in you, and to experience his nearness and embrace his love. Make Psalm 27:4-14 your prayer.

Many Christians struggle with the concept of contentment because they confuse it with complacency. Complacency is rooted in a self-centered disregard for anything or anyone outside of ourselves. When life seems unfair, complacency sits back, unconcerned about the circumstances and unwilling to take action or make changes. But consider the heart of contentment:

- Contentment is not uprooted by the outward changes of life but is anchored in a thankful heart, praising God in the ups and downs of life.

- Contentment is found in God-centric purposes, not egocentric control.

- Contentment turns injustice over to God and rests in his ability to use the raw deals in life to draw us closer to him.

- Contentment actively seeks God, his wisdom, his counsel and his vision for how he will bring about his own good purposes.

- Contentment knows that our abilities rest in Christ who strengthens us.

I'm still learning what it means to be content. But the more I learn, the more I recapture the joy of living. A contented life is not an extravagant life. Rather it's marked by the simplicity of a thankful heart in all circumstances—a heart that sings the prayer of David: "Now, our God, we give you thanks and praise your glorious name" (1 Chronicles 29:13). Out of pure obedience, almost without emotion, like the hallowed statuette, I bow my head and extend my empty heart to God, thanking him for bringing me a step closer to his heart and preparing me to meet him in a new way.

REST STOP

Read God's promises, and determine how he wants to fulfill them in you today (Isaiah 57:14-19; Habakkuk 3:17-19; Zephaniah 3:17 and John 6:48-51).

A Desert Journey

Read Mark 10:46-52, and picture this scene in your imagination:

Bartimaeus pulled his thinning, tattered cloak tighter around his bony shoulders. He hoped to keep the morning chill away as he settled onto the dusty roadside, ready to begin his day of begging for help. No one who traveled the road to or from Jericho was exempt from this blind beggar's cry. But this morning Bartimaeus sensed elevated conversations, feet hurrying by at a quicker pace, and so he called out to no one in particular, "What's going on? Who's coming?"

"It's Jesus of Nazareth," a passerby yelled. Bartimaeus had heard of Jesus and had hoped beyond hope to meet this common man with uncommon powers. No time to waste, he filled his lungs with air, his heart with faith and began to cry out in his loudest voice, "Jesus, Son of David, have mercy on me!" Over and over his cries rose above the din of voices, past the people who at one time or another had tossed coins his way.

Outraged and embarrassed by this roadside spectacle, many townspeople tried to hush the old man, not wanting to bother their famous visitor who had so honored and blessed their town. But Bartimaeus would not relent. In fact, panicked that he would be silenced, he shouted all the more, "Son of David, have mercy on me!"

Then, a calming quiet fell over the crowd. Bartimaeus strained to hear the words being spoken, but he missed the tender voice of Jesus that said to those gathered around, "Call him." The crowd parted as one man looked toward Bartimaeus's expectant face and said, "Cheer up! On your feet! He's calling you." Before anyone could even offer him a hand or lead him down the path, Bartimaeus jumped to his feet with uncharacteristic energy. He threw off his cloak and, with arms extended, shuffled down the dusty road toward the Master.

Jesus reached for Bartimaeus and asked with all sincerity, "What do you want me to do for you?" A smile slowly spread across Bartimaeus's wrinkled face. Never had anyone asked him such an outrageous question. In fact, if

*someone had stopped on any given day and asked him, "What do you want
me to do for you?" he could have thought of a hundred different things. Perhaps he would have answered, "Just sit near me, and let's talk." Or maybe he
would have said, "Describe this fragrant tree and the bird that sings from it."
But Jesus' question astonished him. And all Bartimaeus wanted at that moment was to see the face of the one who cared enough to ask the question and
held power enough to fulfill the request. And so with slow, deliberate words
he whispered, "Rabbi, I want to see."*

*A simple cry from an empty beggar, a simple question from one full of
mercy and love, a simple answer full of faith, and, just like that, light pushed
through the dark. Bartimaeus squinted and shielded his eyes at first. But realizing that the healing power of God was now flooding through his heart,
all he could do was bow down and receive the gift that Jesus offered. Never
again would he cling to the tattered cloak around his shoulders or grab for
coins tossed at his feet. Never again would he rely on the pity of others to
provide for his needs. For now he knew complete satisfaction and joy pouring down from the Father of the heavenly lights as Jesus said to him, "Go,
your faith has healed you."*

HIDDEN JOY

Consider the meditation on the story of Bartimaeus, and
record your thoughts in your journal:

- In what ways do you relate to Bartimaeus? He tossed aside his
  tattered cloak, left his strategic location at the city gate and
  tuned out the expectations of others. What things in your life
  do you need to set aside, leave behind or tune out in order to
  receive the gifts of Jesus? In what ways did Bartimaeus embrace
  the moment given him? What did it require him to do?

- Pray the prayer of Bartimaeus. Let your heart run to Jesus when
  you sense him close at hand. Listen to his outlandish question

as he asks you, "What do you want me to do for you?" Then answer with a heart full of faith, "Let me see your face; let me see my emptiness; let me see my false comforts as the rags that they are; let me receive your strength to cast it all aside as you fill my empty basket with your healing gift of contentment."

- Read the story immediately preceding the one of Bartimaeus in Mark 10:35-45. How are these stories similar? How do James's and John's attitudes differ from Bartimaeus's? Why were James and John unable to receive what they asked for? How did their request affect the other disciples? How did Jesus redeem this situation? Have your self-centered requests and expectations negatively affected those around you?

- Put aside your books, your journal, even your Bible for a period of time. Pray again the phrase from Psalm 86:11, "Give me an undivided heart." Be still before God, and be at rest in his silence. Let his Spirit impress your mind and embrace your heart as you learn to be content in the cloak of his stillness.

2

REST . . .

in the Desert of Weariness

It is not necessary to have great things to do. I turn my little omelette in the pan for the love of God; when it is finished, if I have nothing to do, I prostrate myself on the ground and adore my God, Who gave me the grace to make it, after which I arise, more content than a king. When I cannot do anything else, it is enough for me to have lifted a straw from the earth for the love of God.

BROTHER LAWRENCE,
THE PRACTICE OF THE PRESENCE OF GOD

QUIET YOUR HEART

Read Lamentations 3:19-26. Regardless of your current circumstances today, spend a few minutes calling to mind God's faithfulness and love in your life thus far. Thank him for his compassion. Express your hope as you wait for him to reveal himself in a new way today.

ENTER HIS PRESENCE

Read Psalm 136. Consider how God's enduring love permeates every thought, action and circumstance. Write your own psalm in the style of Psalm 136, but use the list of God's faithful acts that you recalled in the exercise above. Read your song of praise aloud to God.

I LOOKED BACK OVER MY CALENDAR FROM LAST YEAR, and it made me feel good. I'd been productive in a meaningful sort of way—investing in others' lives. Folded into my active family life, I'd written two books and numerous articles, taught a variety of groups, traveled some and attended conferences. My fruitfulness allowed me to reap a deep satisfaction in what I had accomplished.

But that was last year. On this day, I couldn't even muster the inspiration to write a decent paragraph for the church newsletter. I felt soul-weary, depleted of creativity and even of the desire to "produce." My journal reflected my dilemma:

> Today the words refuse to come. They're stuck deep down inside—a cough of a phrase, a stuttering syllable, starts and stops with no beginning or end. Where's the flow, where's the rhythm? The drummer that beats is neither different nor familiar. He is simply gone. Have I no thought, no idea or opinion to express? I begin to wonder but realize I don't know what to wonder about.

Empty was the only word I could come up with to describe my feeling. So I put aside my work and the attempts to will myself into production. Sometimes, following seasons of fruitfulness, we find ourselves inexplicably in a desert, burned out by the burst of activity. As I entered this dry and unproductive place, I should have contented myself to lean back into the much-needed stillness descending upon me, to let it seep in and restore my soul. But I'm not a patient rester. I cry like a child, "Can I get up now? I'm not tired. I don't want to rest." I can relate to Elijah hiding in the cave. The whirlwinds, fire and earthquakes in life do not surprise me. But when God comes in stillness and whispers his love, I sometimes want to cover my head, unsure of what to make of his tender presence and his call to come and rest.

What a paradox that while we long for a break from the weariness of work, we rail against rest in our society. We want to work harder to gain more so we can retire early and enjoy life. And yet we feel guilty when we take time off, worrying that people will think we're lazy, or that someone or something will pass us by and we'll lose our competitive edge. Our American heritage doesn't encourage rest. The work ethic, instilled at the birth of our nation, calls us to conquer all and reach all. Today we charge into action with the battle cry of "Just do it!"—a modern twist on three American ideals:

The pursuit of happiness. It's the inalienable right of all Americans, first claimed in our Declaration of Independence. Unfortunately there was no attached "happiness map" to tell us how to get there or an X to show us when we've arrived. The pursuit of happiness never ends, and Americans travel to every extreme to find it.

Manifest destiny. Conquer and possess the land, from sea to shining sea. If it's within reach, take it. We may think this ideal no longer applies since we have fulfilled that destiny. But in everyday life, we stake our own claims to get more: We trade in the

economy car for an SUV. We can't settle for middle management when there's upper management to conquer. We don't
even order an old-fashioned burger and fries without proclaim-
ing, "Super-size it!" We may not call it manifest destiny any
longer, because we've replaced the concept with the politically
correct term "upward mobility." Like the proud people at the
Tower of Babel, we too strive to reach higher and go farther.

Failure is not an option. This phrase, made popular by the
heroic mission of Apollo 13, reminds us that we can accomplish
anything we set our minds to—even reach the moon. Our in-
genuity enables us to conquer all obstacles at any expense. Simply believe in yourself, and you will embrace success and
satisfaction in your work.

The result of our attitude about work and rest frustrates us
as we realize that it all leads us back to a place called Weary. We
can't live up to the American Dream. The pursuit of happiness
often leads us down dead-end streets. We feel that we're losing
ground instead of gaining it. And if "failure is not an option,"
then what are we to do with the reality of our mistakes and fall-
en expectations?

The load of such disappointment bends us over and beats us
down physically, spiritually and emotionally. We sense that
something is out of balance because we don't have enough energy or motivation to do everything that needs to be done.
Even if we could handle it all, it wouldn't be with the excellence
and satisfaction that we'd like.

We think if we could just get away and take a breather, we'd
feel better and work harder. We try to create our own rest and
retreats, but we often leave those places weary at the thought
of returning to our daily tasks. So all we hope for and pray for

is that we'll make it from one scheduled break to the next without losing our sanity.

REST STOP

When have you felt overloaded or burned out by work? Which of these three American ideals best fits your own work ethic? Describe how you feel when you sense a need for rest in your life. What circumstances lead you to that feeling? Read Psalm 55:4-8. How do you relate to David's words? Turn these words into your prayer to express your need for rest.

RIVERS OF DELIGHT

One of the most quoted passages from the Bible is Jesus' call to come and rest. Its popularity may lie in our continued longing to drink from this well of Living Water. In the Amplified Bible, Matthew 11:28-29 reads like this: "Come to me, all you who labor and are heavy-laden and overburdened, and I will cause you to rest [I will ease and relieve and refresh your souls.] . . . and you will find rest (relief and ease and refreshment and recreation and blessed quiet) for your souls."

Jesus offers deep, refreshing rest, yet we rarely enjoy it. Maybe then our dilemma lies not in our failure to understand rest but in how to embrace work. Perhaps Jesus is saying, "When you work and feel burdened, let me come to that place of labor and join you. Let me make it a sacred and holy place." When I stop trying to make God into a repair kit for my work life, then I can invite him to simply *be* my life. Jesus models for us how to renew our minds and attitudes so that we can learn a better way to embrace work and find rest in doing so.

Be gentle and humble. In the same Matthew passage, Jesus tells us to "learn of me." And what do we learn about Jesus as he worked? He says, "I am gentle and humble in heart" (Matthew 11:29). Not exactly the mindset of corporate America if you want to get ahead. In fact, Jesus' life may best be defined as "downward mobility"—from heavenly immortality to human frailty. And in his humanity, he didn't flaunt his birthright to exalt himself but used it to humble himself to reach and touch the outcasts and the fringes of society. Then, finally, he laid himself on a cross and hung as a common criminal. He accomplished the task set before him by resisting the temptation to exalt himself according to the world's standards.

Brother Lawrence, a monk who lived at the end of the sixteenth century, exemplified what it means to work with a gentle and humble heart. He found his simple, ordinary work to be the most effective means to know God: "Our actions should unite us with God when we are involved in our daily activities, just as our prayer unites us with Him in our quiet time.... Never tire of doing even the smallest things for Him, because He isn't impressed so much with the dimensions of our work as with the love in which it is done."[1]

Discover the joy in work. The first time we meet God in Genesis, he is already busy at work, ordaining, creating and forming. In the magnificence and excellence of his work, he reveals that same gentle and humble heart by imparting his glory into his creation and delegating his power to man. The first thing he intended for humanity was to know him and join him at work. Certainly God could have named the animals and cared for the garden himself, yet this was something he knew man would enjoy, and so he shared that joy with him. He allows us to sense his presence and find satisfaction in the act of creating, ordaining and forming a life in unity with our Maker. When we seek to please God and to unite ourselves with him in the work he has ordained, then we can pray the words of Jesus, "By myself I can do nothing . . . for I seek not to please myself but him who sent me" (John 5:30).

View work as sacred. In the midst of our work, we, like Moses, can find holy ground. It fascinates me that our Bible heroes performed work of all kinds. Moses was herding sheep when God spoke to him. Gideon was threshing wheat, and Elisha was plowing a field when God redirected their lives. Amos was a shepherd and kept a sycamore and fig orchard. Lydia was a dealer of purple fabric. The faithful centurion was in charge of a hundred soldiers. At least four of the apostles were involved in the fishing industry. Matthew was a tax collector, and Jesus was a carpenter. God valued the profession of each of these individuals enough to mention them in their life stories found in Scripture. For it was in such places of work that God met them and prepared them for his special calling.

So it should be with us. It doesn't matter if our work requires us to clean toilets or create art, wait tables or preach sermons. The work becomes sacred because God has delegated it to our realm of authority. When we go to our workplaces with him on our minds and in our hearts, we will experience rest while we work rather than feel a desperate need to get away from it all. "God's sovereignty isn't abstract—it's a working sovereignty and is expressed in work. All of our work is intended as an extension of and participation in that sovereignty."[2]

Some may worry that this new attitude of resting in God will diminish the quality of work or the effort put into it. However, just the opposite is true. When we truly have God at our side, when we "promote him" to Lord of our workplace, our quality should increase. We've released the imperfect boss and embraced the one who is wise and competent and excellent in all ways. We become more excited and motivated to work for him and give him our best.

Our role in our labor is the same as it is in our rest—to become that open channel. For when God is the director of our days of work, and when he is present in the hours of our rest, we find joy in the midst of it all and avoid the conflicts of imbalance and overcommitment. And this moves us from work to faith, from religion to relationship and from knowledge to devotion. It puts rest into our work.

REST STOP

Which new attitude about work seems the most challenging to you and why? Read John 6:27-29. What new attitude about work does Jesus express here? How would these new ideas change the stress level of your work environment? How might God be using your work as a place to speak to you?

In addition to new attitudes about rest and work, God also provides tools to help us grasp the kind of rest he refers to in Matthew 11—that even when we are worn out from work, we're at rest in him; and even when we rest, we're at work with him.

SABBATH REST

Learning to find rest in the midst of work helps lessen the fatigue factor, but there comes a time when we are called to set aside the work and enter into Sabbath rest—one day each week set aside as hallowed and sacred. It's a holy day given over to God and a day that God has given over to us as a gift. When we cease from our work routines, we're able to rest, reflect and see the beauty of what God has allowed us to create and accomplish. Following each day's work during the creation, God did this very thing. He rested from it, observed it and enjoyed it. Then he proclaimed it was good, and it was very good. So too when we enter a Sabbath rest, we cease our striving, we take time to reflect on life, and we find ways to enjoy simply being alive.

Why is it so important to practice a Sabbath rest? Because it strips away all that calls us to leave God's side. It silences the enticements to seek satisfaction and comfort from our work on our own. And it quiets our fantasy that we can accomplish alone anything we set out to do, even the earning of our salvation. In her book *Listening for God* Renita Weems writes:

> Once upon a time, Sunday was a special day, a holy day, a day different from the other six days of the week. It was enough to spend six days a week trying to eke out a living, worrying about whether you were ahead or behind, fretting over the future, despairing over whether life would ever get better. . . . Six days of worrying was enough. The Sabbath was the Lord's Day, a momentary cease-fire in our ongoing struggle to survive and an opportunity to surrender ourselves to the rest only God offered. Come Sunday we set aside our worries about the mundane and renewed our love affair with eternity.[3]

Renewing "our love affair with eternity" refocuses our world and refreshes our minds. We desperately need these times of stillness, and even solitude, for two reasons. First, it rehabilitates our hearts through rest, recovery and perspective.[4] We al-

low our bodies to physically rest from the clamor and demands
of our world. We allow our minds to recover from the barrage
of information. When these two aspects of healing occur, we
are in the right posture to receive God's perspective on life.

Second, stillness and rest habilitate our hearts. Webster's
defines *habilitate* as to make fit or capable; to clothe, dress, to
qualify oneself. As we come to God in silence, he is the one
who prepares us for the journey ahead that we cannot see. We
are clothed in his righteousness, dressed by his love. In silence
we put on the full armor of faith. In this stillness God pre-
cedes us and prepares us for the days ahead, qualifying us
through his grace and mercy for the challenges and trials that
inevitably come.

THE CHURCH

The second tool of rest God gives us is the church, his body.
Here we have the ability to take a burden from one and distrib-
ute the weight among others. Recently a grieving friend called
and talked about her mother's death for a long time. Her burden and pain had affected her ability to work or rest. But family
after family from our church came to help care for her children,
cook meals, wash clothes, clean house and do whatever needed
to be done.

That night our conversation remained fresh on my mind. As
I tossed and turned, I spent the time praying for her. I sensed
God telling me that for this one night, perhaps my friend rested easier than she had in days, because the church was able to
bear some of her burden in Jesus' name. And I began to see it
as a privilege to lie awake for her and pray for her.

It may seem a bit inconvenient to lose a night's sleep over

someone else's problem or to care for another family when we have our own to tend to, but God created his church to function in this way (Colossians 3:12-17). When we participate in the body and intentionally connect ourselves with God's people, we find an increased sense of rest and comfort even as we shoulder the heavy burdens of life.

REST STOP

Take time to ask God what changes you need to make in your life in order to experience Sabbath rest. Read Ephesians 4:22-24. What old attitude does God ask you to cast off, and what new idea must you put on?

When we look at the reality of weariness or rest, the choice to accept Christ's invitation doesn't seem hard. Yet it requires that we die to ourselves and live for Christ. When we begin to do that, our new attitudes and tools for work and rest will help us realize these truths:

- Weariness results when I segment life into pieces—"This part is mine, that part is God's"—rest comes when I listen for God and invite him into every aspect of life, even my work (Colossians 3:22-24).

- Weariness looks at mistakes and disappointments as failures and embarrassments. Rest considers them God's business and his teaching tools (Romans 8:28).

- Weariness says, "If I want it done right, I'll have to do it myself." Rest says, "The only way to accomplish a task is through the strength of Christ and by his grace (Philippians 4:13).

- Weariness refuses to cease working for fear of losing ground. Rest embraces God's delight and enjoyment of all that has been produced.

God allowed me a time of rest to reassess my work habits and my source of motivation. During my desert days, I relinquished the struggle to prove myself competent and embraced God's competence. I let go of my need to perform to human expectations and turned to God for direction and approval. And in the process, I regained the joy in knowing that God's faithfulness provides for my every need.

A DESERT JOURNEY

Read 1 Kings 19, and meditate on Elijah's story as it relates to work and rest.

Queen Jezebel had spoken, and word had been sent to Elijah. He was a wanted man. He walked to the edge of a lean-to shelter, watched the rain and wondered if he had been wrong to humiliate the priests of Baal and then have them all put to death. But God had spoken, and he could no longer tolerate the idolatry and blasphemy from the lips of his chosen people.

"Lord, have you no message for this wicked queen who threatens your sole-surviving prophet? Have you no words for her court and kingdom? Say the word, and I will obey. I am your messenger." Elijah offered up his prayer toward the wet heavens, but all he received was silence and a few drops of rain on his gray beard. The voice of the Lord he understood and recognized. But this silence? What did it mean? Fear and doubt captured his heart, and all he could think to do was run for his life.

Grabbing only his cloak and staff, he raced nearly a hundred miles and then another day's journey into the desert of Damascus. Exhausted physically, emotionally and spiritually, he dropped into the spotty shade of the desert broom bush. Although God's silence remained, Elijah couldn't help but speak to the only one he'd ever known would listen. "I've had enough, Lord. Take my life." Then he lay beneath the scrub brush, praying God would honor this last request from his faithful servant.

How long he slept, he did not know. A gentle tapping on his shoulder jolted him back into his fears. He saw no one but remembered a voice commanding, "Get up and eat." Was it a dream? He was about to rest his head again, but there, near his rolled up cloak, a warm cake and a cool jar of water sat on a flat stone. As was his custom, Elijah blessed the bread, thanked the Lord and ate. Then he lay down to sleep once again. A second time, a presence woke him and provided food and water. This time his strength returned. He knew the hand of the Lord when he saw it. He sensed God was preparing him for a long desert journey.

The food and rest revived his soul, but still he felt weary of heart. Elijah picked up his staff and cloak and headed into the desert. Forty days he traipsed through the sand and scrub, the heat and hills, unsure of where he was or why he was there until he stood at the foot of a mighty mountain. Then he knew. The Spirit of God had led him to this place. All the days that seemed so barren and silent, God was always leading, always gently nudging him forward and providing strength. Now at the foot of Mt. Horeb, the mountain of God, he began to ascend to the place where God had met with Moses in a burning bush. Higher and higher he climbed until he came to a cave and entered in, bone tired.

As he rested in this place, he sensed God's nearness, and finally the voice of the Lord came to him. Elijah yielded his heart and invited the Lord to reveal his message. But something was different. This message was not one to be delivered, but rather one to be received by Elijah himself: "What are you doing here, Elijah?" And with great relief, he poured out his heart, his fear and his weariness to God.

"Come out of the cave, Elijah, and I will reveal myself to you." But even before he could rise from the ground, the power of the Lord sent an incredible wind that shattered rocks and tore away plants. Elijah retreated further inside and waited. Then the earth began to tremble, and fire engulfed the mountain and leapt across rocks. Still Elijah waited. After the cataclysm of nature, he knew the Lord Almighty had arrived.

Elijah smiled at the irony that the all-knowing, all-wise and all-powerful God, who controls the wind and fire, and who created the heavens and earth, would come to a weary and frightened old man in the voice of a gentle whisper. How it soothed his heart and comforted his worried mind. And so he rose and, in humility, covered his face with his cloak and stepped toward the mouth of the cave as God had instructed.

Again God whispered not a prophetic message to deliver to a kingdom, not a command of wrath to be brought down on a nation but a private message of refreshment out of his concern for Elijah's spirit. And God asked again, "Elijah, what are you doing here?" Sensing the deep love and concern from his master, Elijah poured out his heart, his complaints and his feelings of defeat in bringing Israel fully back to their God.

God had refreshed Elijah physically under the broom tree in the barren desert and spiritually through this mountaintop meeting. But still he knew of Elijah's emotional emptiness, and he revealed his plan to bring others alongside him as support, to carry out duties and to encourage him in his work. Touched by the tender heart of a powerful God, Elijah went back through the desert refreshed, as he remembered God's promises and prophecies not only for a nation but also for one weary man.

HIDDEN JOY

Consider the story of Elijah, and record the ideas and thoughts that affected you the most. Then answer these questions in your journal:

- God provided rest for Elijah physically, spiritually and emotionally. Where do you see your biggest need for rest in your life?

- Even though Elijah was doing God's work, he suddenly appeared weary and worn out. Why? Consider the work Elijah continued to do even in his weakness and in his rest. How have you noticed God's presence in your work world? In what ways did Elijah completely surrender to the Lord? Do you think Elijah felt rested after this experience? Why or why not?

- Ask God to give you a personal message of rest or comfort. Then sit quietly and listen with your heart.

- Read 1 Kings 17:1-6. God again provides food and water to Elijah. How are these circumstances different from those previously described in chapter 19? How is Elijah's state of mind different from his desert experience? Consider that God's faithfulness and provision does not depend on our emotional state. How have you seen God's hand at work in times of need and in times of ease in your own life? Reread Lamentations 3:19-26 as your praise to God.

- Read John 5:16-45. How do Jesus' thoughts reflect his work ethic? How can you implement these concepts and truths into your life? Chose some of Jesus' words in this chapter and rewrite them as your prayer to help you experience rest in your work.

3

IDENTITY . . .

in the Desert of Confusion

Our souls were created in the image and likeness of God. . . .
How unfortunate that we do not really understand ourselves
. . . because we so seldom consider the nature and quality of our
inner life.

TERESA OF ÁVILA, *THE INTERIOR CASTLE*

QUIET YOUR HEART

Read Ephesians 3:14-21 as your prayer. Ask the Lord to strengthen your inner being through his Spirit. Consider how his love has rooted your life and established your path. Consider the dimensions of Christ's love for you today.

ENTER HIS PRESENCE

Read Psalm 16:5-11. Meditate on God's sovereignty in laying out the path of life for you. Praise him for his counsel, his wisdom and his willingness to lead you each step of the way.

I MAKE A DECENT LIVING SELLING INSURANCE, BUT I'M just not sure that what I'm doing is what I'm supposed to be doing. Am I really making a difference in this world?" (a middle-aged man).

"We're trying to decide if we should have another baby. It scares me to think of having four children, but it scares me more to see my kids growing up, leaving me to wonder, 'Who am I without my kids?' I'm not sure I remember. Or maybe I never knew to begin with" (a young mother).

"There are so many choices to make. I'm afraid of making the wrong one and being stuck in some career or with somebody that I shouldn't be with. How do I know what's right?" (a college student).

"It's harder and harder to get around these days. I never thought old age would feel like this. I'm not sure what to do with myself here. I just want to age with grace and leave behind a legacy of faith rather than regret" (a nursing-home resident).

Regardless of age, position or season of life, we all come face to face with the universal fear of living a life without meaning or purpose. We ask ourselves tough questions, hoping to unravel the mystery of who we are. As I walked through my season in the desert, I wondered if I was having a midlife crisis. I remember sitting in a hospital waiting room with my mother while my grandmother was in surgery to remove some of the cancer that had invaded her body. I asked her, "Did you ever feel like I feel—kind of confused or empty about who you are?"

My very settled and contented mother nodded and replied, "I remember feeling restless about myself." I was glad she didn't try to give me answers but simply confirmed that I was not alone and that perhaps I was even on the right track.

I thought I would eventually outgrow this need to search for who I am. But now at forty-something, I have decided I will always peer through a thin fog into my inner being, squinting my eyes to bring into focus what is me, what is God, what is good and what is evil. I want something solid, something I can point a finger toward and say, "This is who I am."

Even as I long to put my hand on a concrete answer to my question, I've learned that it has to be more than this job, that task, this talent or even that spiritual gift. Those things are limited to a brief span of life and subject to human frailty. What I really thirst for is a purpose bigger than me, more lasting than life. I realize that I must let go of myself, my rights and my plans if I'm ever to fully embrace God's vision and become who he intended for me to be. This is the place that author Robert Benson calls "between the dreaming and the coming true." God's vision, since before I was conceived, is his dream of who I am, and my life is the process of turning that dream into reality.[1]

In Scripture we see two disciples grapple with an identity problem (Mark 10:35-45). James and John came to Jesus and said in essence, "In the end, this is what we'd like to accomplish,

Lord, to sit at your side in the kingdom"—a worthy goal, an expression of longing to be at Christ's side, to please him and work with him. But Jesus saw their hearts' desire to identify themselves above all others, to exalt their own position and importance, and he knew such attitudes would keep his followers from knowing God.

So Jesus asked them to reconsider their true identity as his disciples by answering the question, "Can you drink from *my* cup?" What was in his cup? A life of selfless servitude and suffering, and a life lived in full and abundant obedience to the Father. All Christ's attitudes and actions reflect God's glory, and this was his number one purpose. When we long for purpose and passion, we usually end up like James and John—confused but trying hard to find something that makes us feel good, look important or appear productive. Christ draws the line of discipleship at the threshold of the self. And so we continue to struggle with our purpose because the cost of discipleship appears too high.

Finding our true identity in Christ sends us to new levels of commitment where we must search our inner being and discover the interior castle where God dwells within us. In the early sixteenth century, a woman known as Teresa of Ávila vowed to live for God alone, and nothing kept her from it—not even the tortures of the Spanish Inquisition. Considering Teresa's focused vision and sure identity in Christ, we would do well to heed her words on avoiding living an unexamined life.

> We do not see who it is that dwells within us. We do not know
> the spiritual treasure that it is to enjoy communion with him.
> And so we make little effort to guard or nurture the soul's beauty.
> All of our attention is focused on the externals not only . . . of

the body, but the outward demonstration of our faith as well. So we focus on the outer walls of the castle, while within the treasures of heaven lie in waste.[2]

SIGNS OF SEARCHING

How do we look inward while keeping life focused on God? How do we allow the Spirit to "strengthen our inner being," as Paul says (Ephesians 3:16), without becoming self-focused instead? Thinking we are pursuing meaning in life, we suddenly realize we are chasing after our own agenda, and we find it lacking. We want to plant a church, and believe God has lead us to do so, but feel like failures when it doesn't go according to our timetable. We want to minister to pregnant teens but feel angry when our efforts appear fruitless. We want to write books but can't accept the rejection that goes along with the process. And we end up feeling confused rather than clarified.

When I thirst for my identify in the fleeting external realities of life, a sense of emptiness and longing continues to rule over me as expectations fall short and achievements feel hollow. But when I finally arrive at the end of myself, thirsty for something real, I come to the beginning of God. For it is in God alone that we find our true humanity.

> The basic, fundamental condition of our humanity is God. We are created by God. We are redeemed by God. We are blessed by God. We are provided for by God. We are loved by God. Sin is the denial, ignorance or avoidance of that basic condition. *Sin* is the word we use for the perverse will with which we attempt to be our own gods or to make other gods for ourselves. Sin is not essentially a moral term, designating items of wrongdoing; it is a spiritual term, designating our God-avoidance and our god-pretensions.[3]

The problem is that, while we believe that our identity will appear when we "find ourselves," in fact, living for our self alone further hides our uniqueness as God's creation. It's not always easy to spot the sin of self-centeredness. In our society, selfishness is cloaked in normalcy. Our lack of commitment, lack of self-control and lack of compassion fill our newspapers and sear our consciences. We have become a nation of egocentric communities—of one with a constitution based on *my* rights, *my* advancement and *my* comfort.

Perhaps this condition is best described and warned against in ancient writings. In Paul's letter to Timothy he said:

> There are difficult times ahead. As the end approaches, people are going to be self-absorbed, money-hungry, self-promoting, stuck-up, profane, contemptuous of parents, crude, coarse, dog-eat-dog, unbending, slanderers, impulsively wild, savage, cynical, treacherous, ruthless, bloated windbags, addicted to lust, and allergic to God. They'll make a show of religion, but behind the scenes, they're animals. (2 Timothy 3:1-5 *The Message*)

RIVERS OF DELIGHT

Although our selfishness is our greatest weakness and the root of all our sin, we must remember that our self is also our greatest strength. It is in our soul that God predetermined our ability to exercise free will. And without free will, there is no sacrifice of love, no intimate give-and-take in our relationship with our Creator.

Knowing who I am in God's sight gives me pause in the desert to rethink and reclaim the hidden beauty of my being. This is the wonder of dying to self. When I fall into the arms of God, I begin to know myself more deeply and can rejoice in who he created me to be. And here I begin to unlock the treasures of heaven.

I am the image of God. We know these words in our head, but we often miss how they affect our heart. Teresa explains, "Suppose an otherwise normal man was asked, 'Who is your father? . . . What country are you from?' And suppose his reply was, 'I have no idea.' Wouldn't we think this man absurdly ignorant? But isn't our spiritual ignorance just as absurd? So many Christians of 'strong faith' make no attempt to discover their true identity in relation to our King."[4]

This is the seed of our identity from which all other activity and meaning grows. "God created man in his own image, in the image of God he created him" (Genesis 1:27). Rabbi David Wolpe explains that these two reflective statements express two different ideas: "The first half . . . means that each individual is created in that individual's own image. Then we receive the infusion of the Divine spark. In other words, our own uniqueness comes first. We are stamped with the image that will be only ours, and then we receive an ember of God."[5]

When I stop to consider the miracle of my existence and acknowledge the fact that it is only by God's will that I live and move and have my being, then I can begin to glimpse the ways God delights in my physical existence (Acts 17:28). I more fully appreciate the uniqueness of my personality, my smile, my laugh, my thoughts and my dreams. This miracle of being a self-contained, living soul, existing by the breath of God, leads me to proclaim as David did, "I praise you because I am fearfully and wonderfully made" (Psalm 139:14).

I am the beloved bride of Christ. Although the reality of our physical being is miraculous, even more so is what happens to our spiritual being. Paul said it none too delicately, "Though outwardly we are wasting away, yet inwardly we are being renewed day by day" (2 Corinthians 4:16). In other words, even though our body grows old and eventually wears out, our spirit grows more beautiful and vibrant the longer we dwell in relationship with Christ. In 2 Corinthians 3:18 he gives an even more picturesque view of our spiritual beauty when he writes, "And we, who with unveiled faces all reflect the Lord's glory, are being transformed into his likeness *with ever-increasing glory*" (emphasis added).

When I read those words, I picture myself coming toward Jesus as his bride, a veil covering my face. And when I meet with him, he lifts that veil, and I look into his eyes, transformed minute-by-minute by the gaze of his love. It amazes me that a magnificent, holy, light-bearing, radiant God would choose to share that glory with you and me, not just to honor us but to reflect off of us his love for this world. Life then becomes a mirror, a reflector of his glory.

REST STOP

Read Romans 12:1-2. How does this Scripture integrate the physical and spiritual essence of your being? Which aspect of self do you need to ask God to restore to its original beauty through Christ? How do these verses balance what we do with who we are?

I am God's chosen vessel. Sometimes, as I wander through the desert thirsty for answers to the meaning of life, God asks me to rethink how I live and gives me not answers but questions to prod me to relinquish myself and come into the fullness of his purpose. His questions center me on the potter's wheel as he shapes my soul for his glory. I become his vessel as he equips me to love others and to please him. At the end of my day, at the end of my life, I pray I can answer these questions in the affirmative: Have I loved well? Have I pleased God?

What broad latitude love affords us as we relate to God and to the world. "St. John of the Cross once said that 'at the evening of our day we shall be judged by our loving.' As we look back over our day, what we have done is not as important as how we have done it. Better to do little with much love than much with little love. For without love, whatever we do will be dismissed with a judicial wave of heaven's hand as just so many trivial pursuits."[6]

Certainly if we love well, we will please God. Paul tells us that each of us should "find out what pleases the Lord" (Ephesians 5:10). And Jesus himself said, "By myself I can do nothing . . . for I seek not to please myself but him who sent me" (John 5:30). It follows that if my goal is to please God, I am no longer obsessed about pleasing myself, because pleasing God becomes my greatest pleasure. The only way to answer these questions is to take time to look, observe and meditate on my actions and thoughts each day and to turn them again and again toward God's light.

Recently I went to church angry over an injustice committed against my family and me. The man who had harmed us was someone we had helped financially, even providing a place for him to live and welcoming him into our church family. Although he sought our forgiveness and made restitution for the wrong, I still harbored anger toward him.

That morning as I wrestled with my anger, I arrived at church and noticed we would be receiving communion. I sat down and prayed, "God, change my heart and remove the bitterness." Then the man who had wronged us came into the service and sat next to me. Not exactly the answer to prayer I had hoped for. As angry as I should have been, I felt the resentment begin to melt away as I remembered Christ's sacrifice for *my* sin. And that remembrance put me on level playing ground with everyone else, including this man by my side. There's something about sitting shoulder to shoulder with the ones who have wronged us and whom we have wronged that allows us to be joined in the river of life flowing from the blood of Christ. And there we receive both mercy and forgiveness.

Many times as I look over my day, I realize I have neither loved well nor pleased God. And I take those situations to him and seek his mercy and his miracle of forgiveness. Time and again he allows me to learn, and my failure becomes his vessel of redemption as he sets me again on the potter's wheel and continues to shape my life and conform it to Christ's.

REST STOP

Read Ephesians 4:22-24. Ask God to strip away the attitudes of selfish desire that corrupt the beauty of who he created you to be. Close your eyes and picture how he reclothes you with his glory.

God reveals to each of us who we are in Christ. For some, finding identity is a slow, unfolding journey. For others it is a distinct call and quick obedience. For many it is a detoured, bumpy ride, jolting us over our broken expectations then yielding to God's best for us. While I battle to turn my thoughts away from myself and onto the cross of Christ, that fear of living a life without meaning crumbles under the gaze of love as I pray the prayer of Thomas à Kempis:

> Deepen Your love in me, O Lord, that I may learn in my inmost heart how sweet it is to love, to be dissolved, and to plunge myself into Your love. Let Your love possess and raise me above myself, with a fervour and wonder beyond imagination. Let me sing the song of love. Let me follow You, my Beloved, into the heights. Let my soul spend itself in Your praise, rejoicing for love.[7]

At times I still peer through the fog into my inner being. In this life, as Paul says, "we see through a glass darkly." We only "know in part," but it is enough to point to God's love as seen at the cross and say, "This is what I am all about. Because of his great love, I live."

- Identity rooted in Christ seeks not its own glory but lifts him up as Lord of all.

- Identity rooted in Christ seeks not its own comfort but releases compassion into the world.

- Identity rooted in Christ seeks not to do what pleases the self but what pleases God.

- Identity rooted in Christ seeks not to accomplish great things but rests in the great arms of God's love.

A DESERT JOURNEY

Read Luke 19:1-10, and picture this scene in your imagination:

"Loathsome. Arrogant. Cheat." Zacchaeus had heard all the names whispered loud enough for him to hear as he hurried his wiry little body past the crowd. He pushed aside several individuals and even knocked a child to the ground in his haste to be the first to the gate. Deep down he knew the citizens of Jericho hated him, but he pretended that the money and the political clout he carried as chief tax collector of the region had soothed that hurt. And he convinced himself that he needed to meet Jesus, for political reasons.

There was talk that Jesus was headed this way. Loved by the common people, despised by the Pharisees, the preacher fascinated him. Zacchaeus had heard him teach once before and saw him heal dozens of the sick and crippled. But more than that, Jesus spoke a message of God's love for all people, including someone like him. He had even heard that another tax collector was now one of Jesus' chosen disciples. Maybe he could weasel his way into a personal meeting with Jesus. "Might do my reputation some good with the local townspeople," he reasoned.

There was only one problem: he would never see Jesus nor would Jesus see him if he stood around waiting in the crowd. A whole head shorter than the average man, Zacchaeus couldn't see over anyone, so he had made a plan and now hurried past the others. He spotted it up ahead. The sycamore tree by the city gate would be the perfect lookout point. Its low branches provided an easy way to swing his legs up, and he shinnied his way higher.

"I see them coming," he yelled, more as a reflex than a thoughtful gesture to the people below. The announcement sent the crowd en masse through the gates to meet Jesus on the road, and Zacchaeus was left alone in his perch. Certain he would never be seen now, he contented himself to simply observe. Truth be told, he was feeling a bit nervous about his plan. What if Jesus condemned him in front of the townspeople? He considered the scene and manufactured a rebuttal to the accusations. But who could stand against the strong words of the mighty teacher? No doubt Zacchaeus would be made the fool, the brunt of the joke, again. His courage evaporated, and he leaned back against the tree trunk, hoping no one would notice him there.

The crowd was noisy, jubilant and full of hope as they approached the *gate. When Jesus arrived, he stopped directly below the tree. Zacchaeus's heart raced. "Move on, move on," he mumbled to himself. But when Jesus stopped, the crowd stopped, and a hush fell over them as they waited for his words. He looked up, directly into the tree. Zacchaeus wiped his brow, praying he would not be noticed, but he couldn't help looking toward Jesus. He was somehow drawn to his face, and he leaned slightly forward for a peek.*

A smile spread across Jesus' face as he motioned to him, "Zacchaeus, hurry down from there. I must stay with you at your home." Zacchaeus pointed a finger to his own chest as if to ask, "Me?" Jesus nodded, and Zacchaeus was down on the ground next to him in a flash. Some of the crowd began to complain to Jesus about his choice in the company he kept, but Jesus simply put his arm around Zacchaeus's shoulder and headed up the road.

They walked slowly, and most of the crowd dwindled away, disappointed in the object of Jesus' attention on this day. The two men talked and talk. Zacchaeus couldn't remember the last time he'd held a real conversation and someone had actually listened to him. Today he felt ten feet tall as they reminisced about childhood games and tree climbing. They talked of dreams and disappointments and what it is that changes a man from self-seeking to God-seeking.

By the time they reached his home, Zacchaeus had fully given his heart to Jesus. Zacchaeus turned and stood on the top step of the portico, facing the disciples and the few who remained of the crowd. For the first time in a long time he felt a new love toward these people. He had only one purpose in mind, to please his Lord. So he announced to them all, "Here and now, in honor of my Lord and Master, I commit to you all and before God to give half of all my possessions to the poor. And if I have cheated anyone, I will repay them four times what they lost."

Jesus embraced Zacchaeus and then made his own announcement: "Today, salvation has come to this house, because this man too is a son of Abraham. For the Son of Man came to seek and to save what was lost." And Zacchaeus welcomed Jesus, along with the entire crowd at his doorstep, into his home to celebrate.

HIDDEN JOY

- In reflecting on this story, consider what inward changes Jesus made in Zacchaeus's life and what outward changes resulted.

- In what ways have you been changed inwardly as a result of knowing Jesus? How is your physical, tangible world a reflection of these changes? Do they reflect God's purposes?

- Does it matter which comes first: an outward change or an inner, spirit change? Why? How has knowing Christ helped focus your life and give it meaning?

- Read Paul's prayer to the Colossian church in Colossians 1:9-14. Make a list of God's inner work and our outward responses mentioned in this prayer. Which aspect of this prayer do you most need in your own life?

- Read Colossians 3:1-17. What practical suggestions does Paul give to help keep your life focused on God? Where do you normally set your heart in a routine day? What reasons does Paul give for living a holy life? In this passage, what words or phrases stir your heart or convict your spirit?

- Consider taking a sentence or phrase from this passage and rewriting it into a life goal or mission statement. Write it out on an index card and keep it in a place where it can remind you of your focus for a meaningful life.

4

LIGHT . . .

in the Desert of Darkness

Before the soul discovers what is meant by the precious union with God, it is in darkness. True, you may have knowledge of the scriptures, and may have mental agreement with the doctrines of Christ. But until God speaks—"Let there be light!" a thick darkness covers the abyss of every soul.

JOHN OF THE CROSS, *LIVING FLAME OF LOVE*

QUIET YOUR HEART

Read Psalm 107:10, 14-16. Join the psalmist in thanking God for his unfailing love. Imagine yourself in a quiet place of nature with storm clouds hiding the sun. As time passes, the clouds begin to part until eventually you stand in the full light and warmth of God's love. "Restore [me], O God Almighty; make your face shine upon [me], that I may be saved" (Psalm 80:3 paraphrased).

ENTER HIS PRESENCE

Read Psalm 18:11. Consider how darkness and light emanate equally from God. His love and his presence dwell fully in fire and cloud, in shadow and sun, in day and night. Praise him for the ways he inhabits your heart, whether it is currently cloaked in darkness or drenched in light.

IN 1999, BURIED IN THE RUBBLE OF A FALLEN TURKISH city, in a lightless crawlspace no larger than eighteen inches high, lay a four-year-old boy. Tons of cement, bricks, boards and dirt covered him, a result of the earth's upheaval from deep within the ground. Thousands upon thousands of people lost life, home, family and any sense of stability as a result of the earthquake. Six days after the disaster struck, relatives found the boy miraculously alive. Somehow he survived alone in the darkness without food, water or human touch. An uncle, searching for useable remnants of his home, shined a light into the tiny space and found his nephew, emaciated and wide-eyed, but alive. The child summed up his ordeal in whispered simplicity, "I was very scared."

We all suffer through seasons of loss when darkness, fear and doubt shake the foundations of our existence—times when the inner cities we have built and believed to be indestructible go through a great upheaval from deep within our souls. We lie buried beneath the rubble of our broken-down world, wondering if we will ever see the light of day or feel the breath of God reviving our emaciated spirits.

When that great upheaval occurs, we are faced with changes

and challenges we often feel ill-equipped to bear. We cannot identify all the pieces of silence and sadness strewn across the dark and
cramped space where we live—the place where we sift through the
rubble for useable remnants from our inner cities and cry to God
like the psalmist, "Turn your steps toward these everlasting ruins."
(Psalm 74:3). We learn to whisper simple prayers for strength to
live in this land. And we pray, "Lord, if I have to be in a place where
'I'm very scared,' help me do it with grace."

WALKING IN THE DARK

Rarely do a Christ-followers walk through life without reaching chasms of darkness that loom between them and God. At
times it seems that God calls us to enter into his presence by
stepping into that darkness without any assurance that solid
ground will meet our next footstep. The anonymous author of
The Cloud of Unknowing describes the experience like this: "Try as
you might, this darkness and this cloud will remain between
you and your God. You will feel frustrated for your mind will
be unable to grasp him, and your heart will not relish the delight of his love. But learn to be at home in this darkness. . . .
For if in this life you hope to feel and see God as he is in himself, it must be within this darkness and this cloud."[1] These ep-
isodes of lightless living may come to us when doubt, despair or
death intrudes upon life.

   The darkness of doubt questions our faith. In this dark
cloud, we may thirst for relief from our burdens, change in our
circumstances or comfort in our grief, yet God remains silent.
Is he, after all, a cruel God? During such times of wondering,
we begin to consider how faith is played out in the darkness of
doubt. But many, rather than exercise faith, turn their backs on

God and run, some never to return to find out what the substance of their faith is truly made of.

How sad that doubt brings many to abandon their faith when, ironically, it is the darkness that proves God's nearness. Darkness, by its very nature, defines the place where faith lives. As the writer of Hebrews explains, "Faith is being . . . certain of what we do not see" (11:1). Questions enter our minds and may darken our view of God's presence, but God wants us to confront those questions and bring them straight to him like the psalmist did:

> Will the Lord reject forever?
>   Will he never show his favor again?
> Has his unfailing love vanished forever?
>   Has his promise failed for all time?
> Has God forgotten to be merciful?
>   Has he in anger withheld his compassion? (Psalm 77:7-9)

Such questions allow us to be authentic in our relationship with him. For in the midst of our doubts, we begin to ask God to make sense of it all. And that moment of inquiring of God becomes an act of faith.

REST STOP

In what ways have you experienced seasons of darkness in the desert? Reread Psalm 77:7-9. Identify which questions resonate within your own soul. Write out other questions you have for God. Don't be afraid to be honest with God who knows your heart.

The darkness of despair peers into our own emptiness. This darkness may result from broken expectations or depression. Wanting to avoid the pain of life, we may begin to wear masks of denial or perfection. Plastic smiles may hide the truth from some, but rarely do desperate situations leave us in shallow waters. They require that we look deeper into our own souls to enter the darkness that lies within.

Spiritual battles are waged on the soul in these depths of darkness. John of the Cross was a sixteenth-century Christ-follower, deeply devoted to experiencing and teaching the depth of God's love. But it was in the times of darkness and even torture where that flame of love became a consuming fire. In his writings he identified three aspects of spiritual conflict and despair that churn inside the one learning to walk by faith through the "dark night of the soul." First is the temptation of a lustful spirit. In the midst of prayer or ministry, Satan first attacks our human desires of the flesh in order to defeat God's purpose. Second is the presentation of spiritual lies, the shame voices that condemn us and remind us over and over of our mistakes and failings. Finally, a "perverse spirit" may twist God's truth and light with worry about secret motives or religious perplexities and doctrines, which can paralyze our response to grace.[2]

This is the despair Nicodemus may have faced as he came to Jesus in the darkness of the night to protect his own reputation. His great religious knowledge seemed to have twisted his thinking until the purest concept of God's love for the world perplexed him. But Jesus spoke at length to him about darkness and light as he led him, like a child learning to walk, toward God's free gift of grace.

REST STOP

Which of these three aspects of despair have you experienced? Read the story of Nicodemus and Jesus in John 3. Identify all the aspects of darkness (symbolic or otherwise) that touched Nicodemus's life. How did Jesus bring light to Nicodemus? How does this story speak to you in the darkness?

The darkness of dying to self collides with obedience. Experiencing the loss of a loved one can move us into dark days. But more common in our walk with Christ are the choices we must make each day to die to self and walk in the light. In the spiritual realm, our "loved ones" may be power, reputation, money, food, sex, comfort or a host of other "lovers" begging for our attention. God told the Israelites before they entered the Promised Land to make a choice between loving him and loving the world: "I set before you today life and prosperity, death and destruction. . . . Now choose life . . . for the LORD is your life" (Deuteronomy 30:11-20). Pastor M. Craig Barnes writes, "I have become convinced that Christianity is fundamentally an experience in losing the lives of our dreams in order to receive the lives Jesus died to give us."[3]

REST STOP

What "lovers" keep you occupied with yourself and hidden from God? How have other loves controlled you? Ask Christ to put to death those things that keep you from his love. Read Colossians 2:13-15 as an affirmation of his ability and desire to make this a reality in your life.

RIVERS OF DELIGHT

On at least two occasions, I've passed through the dark desert where I faced many questions about myself and about God. But above all, I wondered how someone who had followed hard after God for so long could suddenly lose track of him. The ways I had come to know God and to meet God no longer brought me into his presence. I felt like he had changed all the rules of how our relationship worked, and it was up to me to figure them out for myself. In reality he was asking that I consider moving from a rote relationship into a new depth of understanding and intimacy. I had given the *tools* of devotion priority over *heart* devotion to God himself.

I attempted to stay in his Word, but it is hard to read in the dark. And while I never dreamed I would have to rearrange my spiritual life, in fact, that is what God required. As a result, new truths began to emerge as I came to rejoice in the God of the dark desert.

Truth 1: God exists beyond my emotion. I considered how much I relied on God as an emotional fix. It *felt* good to talk to God. I *felt* satisfied and cared for. But was my emotion the limit of God's reality, of his character or of his purpose? To mold God into an emotional fix belittled his power, glory and holy being.

Author Donald McCullough calls this "the tendency to refashion God into a more congenial, serviceable God." He writes, "The consuming fire has been domesticated into a candle flame, adding a bit of religious atmosphere, perhaps, but no heat, no blinding light, no power for purification. When the true story gets told, whether in the partial light of historical perspective or in the perfect light of eternity, it may well be revealed that the worst sin of the church at the end of the twentieth century has been the trivialization of God."[4]

My feelings alone have come to seem a shallow reason to follow God as I awake each day to his wonders. I marvel over his creative hand at work around me, in me and through me. I am awed by his mighty wisdom and his call to holiness. I will never fully grasp the depths of God in this life, but I continually pray the words of Paul that I may have power "to grasp how wide and long and high and deep is the love of Christ, and to know this love that surpasses knowledge—that [I] may be filled to the measure of all the fullness of God" (Ephesians 3:18-19).

Truth 2: Silence and darkness are the language of prayer. In the midst of darkness and difficult circumstances, the voice of the Spirit speaks in silence. This is the place where words cannot and must not be uttered. Instead God asks us to be still. Stillness is the prayer of the brokenhearted and the dumbfounded, where the native tongue of tears speaks in the barren land of pain. It is the prayer that stops asking questions and sits silently before the almighty God. When we have no strength or even desire to ask *why* or *how long,* we simply wait in the silence and darkness and ask *who.* There we find a heavenly Father, hallowed and holy, with arms open wide.

Truth 3: There is no difference between day and night to God. He lives beyond the limits of time. There is no waking or sleeping. Sunlight is no brighter than moonlight. He exists in darkness and light equally. They both rise out of his creative purposes. When he created light, he gave it equal footing with darkness— both created in perfection, both created with purpose. David expressed this desert truth when he wrote:

If I say, "Surely the darkness will hide me
      and the light become night around me,"
even the darkness will not be dark to you;
      the night will shine like the day,
      for darkness is as light to you. (Psalm 139:11-12)

REST STOP

How can these three truths help you as you dwell in this time of darkness? What other new truths about God have you discovered on your own?

DISCIPLINES IN THE DARKNESS

In addition to reassuring us that darkness is natural and can be life giving, God equips us with three disciplines that act as nightlights to guide us through our season of darkness.

Stillness. "Let him who walks in the dark, / who has no light, / trust in the name of the LORD / and rely on his God. / But now, all you who light fires / and provide yourselves with flaming torches, / go, walk in the light of your fires / and of the torches you have set ablaze. / This is what you shall receive from my hand: / You will lie down in torment" (Isaiah 50:10-11). Stillness silences the need to control, the need to know and the need to make our own light. When we extinguish our self-made torches and stand in the dark stillness, God reaches out his hand to lead us into his true light.

That word *still*, which is found in the oft-quoted psalm "Be still, and know that I am God," is from a Hebrew word that reveals a greater understanding of this discipline (Psalm 46:10). To be still before God means to cease, to draw toward evening, to fail, to leave, to be faint, feeble, idle, slack, slothful and weak.

Like the setting sun at the end of the day, darkness approaches, and I come to the end of my striving and my labor. I find time to rest. So it is with my faith. When I am done striving on my own to work harder, then I can "be still" and unite my heart to God's, agreeing that I am a sinner. I am weak and unable to make it on my own. When my life is in an uproar, when I take on more than I can handle, make poor life choices, fail or am physically exhausted, then I extinguish my own fires and wait on God, the Consuming Fire, to rekindle my spirit with his presence.

REST STOP

Put away all your books, journals and notebooks. Close your eyes, or go outside to a quiet place, and let the darkness wrap around you and cocoon you in stillness. Let go of your struggle to "emerge" from this place of darkness. Simply allow God in to search your heart and mind and purify you with his love.

Clinging. "My soul clings to you; / your right hand upholds me" (Psalm 63:8). Clinging requires that we hang on to God to find the gift of hope. I cling to God's promise that he will never leave me or forsake me. I cling to God's command to "fear not." But the paradox of clinging to God is that I must let go of doubt and fear and stand before God with open hands of relinquishment.

Hope is the nightlight that reassures me that all will be well. As a Christ-follower, hope is always "on." Its soft glow, like a beacon through fog, says, "Hold on. Stay the course." Frederick

Buechner, in *The Hungering Dark,* wrote this prayer that express-es how we cling to God in the dark:

> Lord, Jesus Christ, help us not to fall in love with the night that covers us, but through the darkness to watch for you as well as to work for you; to dream and hunger in the dark for the light of you. . . . Give us back the great hope again that the future is yours, that not even the world can hide you from us forever, that at the end the One who came will come back in power to work joy in us stronger even than death. Amen.[5]

Watch and pray. When Jesus entered the dark night of his soul in the Garden of Gethsemane, he called his disciples into a new discipline of darkness. He asked them to "watch and pray," to be vigilant even when shrouded by shadows. Watch, expecting God to reveal himself. Pray, expecting God to trans-form your heart and increase your faith.

REST STOP

Read the following promises: Ephesians 2:13; Luke 21:19; Ro-mans 5:5; Romans 15:13; 2 Corinthians 9:8 and Philippians 4:6-7. Write out one of these promises and keep it with you through-out the day. Cling to it, memorize it, speak it and pray it. After-ward, consider how those words ministered to you or through you in your daily life.

John of the Cross emerged from his dark night of the soul al-ways vigilant, always expecting and never more certain of God's great love. In the end he said, "It is well for those who find themselves in the dark night of the soul to persevere in pa-tience. . . . Let them trust in God, who does not abandon those who seek God with a simple and right heart, and will not fail to give them what is needed for the road, until he brings them into the clear and pure light of love."[6]

After the great upheaval from deep within, God always rescues us from beneath our own rubble. We see that God has walked with us and dwelt in us. But more than that, we come to understand that in this place we experience rebirth and emerge wide-eyed into a new realm of God's glory, where he shines his light into our small darkness; we find ourselves miraculously alive and ready to live again, for "the darkness is passing and the true light is already shining" (1 John 2:8).

REST STOP

Write a prayer for perseverance in Christ's call to watch and pray. Picture yourself in the desert, hidden in the cleft of a rock. What are the things you're watching for? Express to God those desires, that sacred thirst that keeps you vigilantly expecting his arrival.

A DESERT JOURNEY

Read Matthew 11:1-15 and 14:1-12, and picture this scene in your imagination:

At first the blackness terrified him. He had never experienced this nothingness that hung heavy on his soul. Even in the dark, he closed his eyes to pray or meditate, or perhaps he was trying to shut out the darkness itself. Three times each day guards carried a torch to this prison in the bowels of the palace and slid another formless, nameless excuse for food across the floor to him. Wild locusts and honey would have been a majestic feast compared to the gray mash they gave him to eat. The torch flame revealed a damp stone floor and reminded John of the stench of human waste surrounding him.

His stomach turned as the moaning of other tortured souls filled his ears. Visions of heaven and hell plagued his thoughts.

Without warning, one day a surprising fourth torch was lit. Footsteps approached, and John recognized the faces of two of his dear disciples. Somehow they had found a way to get in to see him. A bribe perhaps? Whatever the means, John began to cry tears of relief at the sight of them. One of them had hidden a hunk of fresh bread in his cloak. The other brought out a small vial of wine. They spoke soothing words and washed his wounds. But perhaps most healing of all were their stories of what Christ was doing in the towns of Galilee. Jesus—John's own cousin. The name melted his heart. He remembered their few days together, his sense of certainty that Jesus was the Messiah, but the darkness of this dungeon played with his mind and cast shadows over his spirit. "Friends, go to him and ask him, 'Are you the one who was to come, or should we expect someone else?'" They left with promises of a quick return.

Days later, true to their word, they returned and reported Jesus' exact words. "John," they said. "Don't doubt. We've seen with our own eyes. The blind receive sight; the lame walk; those who have leprosy are cured; the deaf hear; the dead are raised and the good news is preached to the poor. And Jesus himself said, 'Blessed is the man who does not fall away on account of me.'"

Their words, like the Spirit moving over the face of the deep at creation, brought light and form to John's miserable existence. For the first time in ages, he rested soundly and peacefully. He knew his days were few in this world, but in the heavy blackness of this prison cell he knew that darkness was passing and the true light was already shining.

Hidden Joy

- When have your convictions about the certainty of God in your life changed to some level of doubt? What are the things that push you toward the darkness of doubt? How have you overcome those doubts?

- What areas of your own life seem dark, formless and void right now? Read Genesis 1:1-5. How might this be a picture of God at work in you?

- John's disciples bore witness to Jesus' healing work. How does evidence of Christ at work in others help us live through the dark times? Read 1 John 1:1-4. Where and how can we find this assurance in our lives? Who has testified of Christ to you, and how has it affected you?

- Read Luke 23:44-49. How does this passage on the death of Jesus reveal God at work in darkness and in light?

- Read 1 John 1:8—2:14. What does this passage present that can help us experience the light of Christ? What are signs that we are failing to live fully in that light of Christ? Offer a prayer to God based on your meditation on these verses.

5

RENEWAL . . .

in the Desert of Loss

*Waiting must and can be the very breath of our life, a
continuous resting in God's presence and his love, a constant
yielding of ourselves for Him to perfect His work in us.
Let us once again listen and meditate until our hearts say with
new conviction: "Blessed are they that wait for him!"*
(Isaiah 30:18).

ANDREW MURRAY,
THE BELIEVER'S SECRET OF WAITING ON GOD

QUIET YOUR HEART

Read Psalm 130. Plan to rise early in the morning, before the sun is up. As the
darkness fades and the light washes over the sky, turn your thoughts to waiting
on the Lord's arrival in your own heart, where the light of his glory pushes
through your own darkest thoughts. Sit in the brilliance of his being, and revel in
his ability to renew your spirit today.

ENTER HIS PRESENCE

Read Psalm 138:7-8. Personalize these verses as a prayer in your journal. Meditate
on the fact that regardless of your circumstances, God is able to fulfill his purposes,
his promises and the desires of your heart. There is reason to rejoice, for his love
endures forever.

As I hit my early forties, I entered a season when I felt stuck spiritually and emotionally, unable to engage the gears that make life turn and advance. Emotion and purpose drained away. In their place a spirit of starkness came calling. Outward losses tumbled over my world as inward loss buried my soul. I often grieved over the changes I faced as I released routines and comforts that had been my life's framework. I said goodbye to loved ones and friends as they slipped from life to death; I came to grips with my crumbling marriage; I left behind my stay-at-home lifestyle and reentered the work world. And though I held hands with loss and death, both great and small, I also realized that beneath the surface of change hides the mystery of new beginnings.

No one escapes the inevitability of change or the pain that often tags along behind it. From the moment of our birth we face it, first by leaving the warmth and security of the womb, and then by learning to live with change as a companion on our walk with God. Although we may face loss, it's more difficult to embrace it and to allow God to wield it as a honing tool for our spirits.

Naomi was a woman who trekked through the desert lands

of change with her daughter-in-law Ruth. One of the first things we read about her is that she was "left without her two sons and her husband" (Ruth 1:5). But rather than hurry off to a happier place and time, Naomi waited on God's provision as she unpacked her loss and draped it like a cloak over her life. She even wanted to change her name to one befitting her situation. "Call me Mara, because the Almighty has made my life very bitter" (Ruth 1:20).

We too move through times when we are left without. We may be left without employment or financial security. We can be left without our health or our dreams, or perhaps without our homes and our families. All these changes may bring us to a desert where we crawl into this place of loss and stop, cocooned in the silence and darkness. Then we finally learn to wait as God uses the losses and subsequent changes of life to transform us and renew us.

We may try to rush out of the pain of loss, or even tiptoe around it, but it is no sleeping giant. It storms into our lives like a dust storm marching across the desert floor, sometimes stirring up so much dirt and dust that it makes it difficult to breathe. It tears up what has settled on the floor of our inner life, uprooting it like tumbleweed sent scurrying across the plains. So in the desert we must wait for the changes themselves to change until we can breathe, relieved that new life is emerging.

Henri Nouwen writes, "The spiritual life is, first of all, a patient waiting, that is, a waiting in suffering, during which the many experiences of unfulfillment remind us of God's absence. But it is also a waiting in expectation which allows us to recognize the first signs of the coming of God in the center of our pains. . . . It is in the center of our longing for the absent God that we discover his footprints."[1]

REST STOP

In what ways have you been left without? How has this affected you emotionally, physically and spiritually?

I hate to admit it, but I once waited in line for over two hours on a blistering July afternoon in Phoenix just to be one of the first people to get a "free" bobble-head doll at a major league baseball game. I tell people I did it as a favor for a friend, but deep down I wanted that dumb doll. So I suffered in the heat in order to get one. But as I stood in line, I realized that my waiting, along with some ten thousand other baseball fans, wasn't true waiting. We all came equipped to endure that afternoon with our own methods for comfort. We brought lawn chairs, water bottles, umbrellas and coolers full of refreshments. We thought we could survive the wait, but even with our battery-operated fans, tempers flared as people packed into lines and stepped over one another.

Not everyone was patient or considerate of others. There was a lot of eye-rolling, foot-tapping and arms-folded waiting that released irritated sighs and head-shaking disbelief that someone would have the gall to make us wait in the heat of the day for so long. And as I observed our behavior, I thought, *This isn't waiting at all. It's a haughty pride and an insistence that the world operate on my speed, by my standards, according to my demands, and, through it all, that my right to be comfortable and receive good service be upheld.*

If it is that hard to wait for something as trivial as a bobble-head doll of a baseball hero, then how do I abide the sacred call to "wait on the Lord" through the upheavals of life? Author Sue Monk Kidd describes her battle with waiting on God: "I had to face the fact that my inability to wait was symptomatic of something amiss in my soul. I feared waiting because such pauses in life brought me close to the dark holes and empty pockets inside me, the rigidities and self-lies I had fashioned."[2]

Our difficulties with this discipline lie in three areas: First, we are not a patient people, willing to wait on God's provision of wisdom, justice and grace. Second, we are not an observant people, willing to wait for God's presence as seen in the ordinary events of our days. And third, we are not a submissive people, willing to wait for God's instruction. We want instant and constant gratification, and we want it with less effort. We are willing to settle for second best as we replace God with material idols. We want to express our anger in revenge and exert our rights in self-centered demands. All these natural reactions to change and loss leave us unsettled, grabbing for control to make things happen when we want them to happen.

But at the core of all our wants—and so often we miss this— is our need for God. We were created to worship, and so God placed within us all a pilot light of his love, hidden beneath the surface of our souls. He waits to strike a holy match to ignite our lives with his passion, but few are willing to open their hearts and turn the tiny flicker toward God's consuming fire. Instead we want to control our own flame, and so we end up living passionless, lukewarm lives of self-indulgence, satisfied with silly trinkets of distraction.

This is what happened to the Israelites while Moses went to the mountain with God to receive the Ten Commandments. They wanted a god who would satisfy *now*. Their hearts were made to worship, but they could not tolerate the wait. So they began to fashion an idol out of gold—something they could dance around in the desert, something that would shine and give them a sense of power and control. That was before they encountered the living and jealous God who is accustomed to waiting for his rebellious people to turn to him and love him with undivided, fully devoted hearts.

REST STOP

In what ways have you failed to wait on God in the past? What has been the result? Write down your frustration with the discipline of waiting on God. Offer that frustration to him in prayer. Ask him to teach you to understand more fully how to wait and trust and rest in his provision, his instruction and his presence.

RIVERS OF DELIGHT

Anytime change occurs, there is always a time, if even for a moment, when life as we know it stops and new life begins. It happens in all of nature, and it is a holy moment of renewal. For the desert locust, that moment occurs when it stops its flying, ceases its buzzing and clings to a tree to shed its skin. A hard, transparent shell—a perfectly formed locust carcass—is left hanging on the tree, a symbol of shedding the old for the new.

We are no different than the locust. Loss is sometimes thrust upon us and sometimes purposely chosen, as we leave behind old ways and start down new paths. So it is with our inner spirit as well. God is not silent about this process, and it is not just a one-time event. The apostle Paul calls us to "put off the old self and put on the new" (Ephesians 4:22-24 paraphrased). But if we, as Christ-followers, have not yet learned how to wait, then it will be difficult to be truly changed and to experience renewal of life every day.

So what then does it mean to wait on God, and how do we learn to do it? Waiting on the Lord is a call to deeper devotion. It's looking for, hoping in and expecting to see God at work in me and around me. But maybe, more precisely, waiting on God is a discipline most needed when I fail to see God close at hand, when I'm cocooned in the losses draped over my life. It's when I'm tempted to reach for false comfort, when my heart wants to rebel or panic and take spiritual shortcuts, that I must simply trust that he is at work in me, around me and through me.

It takes two qualities to wait on God. Psalm 40:1-3 identifies the first quality as patience. "I waited patiently for the Lord; he turned to me and heard my cry." And the second quality is quietness: "It is good to wait quietly for the salvation of the Lord" (Lamentations 3:23-26). Peter describes these virtues as reflected in "the holy women of the past." These were the women whose unfading beauty came from the inner self through a gentle and quiet spirit and who put their hope in God, an often-used phrase for waiting on God (1 Peter 3:3-5).

Waiting on God is not just a motionless, meaningless game we play with God. Waiting, in the Hebrew language, is an active word that calls us to trust, to adhere to God's call and to be entrenched in it, like being carved into wood. It requires a binding and twisting of my heart with God's. Waiting on God is the process of making room for him. I reserve not just a spot for God but my whole heart for him alone to dwell in.

Waiting prepares the way, as John the Baptist did for the Messiah, in the wilderness of my heart. It makes straight paths for my King to enter. I don't want him to have to jump over garbage I've left in the way or obstacles that hide my heart and make it more difficult to enjoy his presence. I want to give him a clear and unfettered pathway to my heart and through my mind.

Devoted waiting on God requires practice in order to experience the joy that God has in store for us. At the turn of the nineteenth century, Andrew Murray, a pastor in South Africa, prayed continually for the renewal and revival of his country. And though revival came in a mighty force by the hand of God, it is Murray's life of devotion and his patient waiting on God that is best remembered, and which prepared him and his country for revival. His was the kind of life that prayed, "Lord, make me as holy as a forgiven sinner can be made; keep me as near to you as it is possible for me to be; fill me as full of your love as you are willing to do . . . on thee do I wait all the day."[3]

Humbled waiting teaches us to posture our hearts to relinquish, receive and worship. And through these acts of devotion, through a metamorphosis of separation, transformation and emergence, God moves us to renewal.

Relinquish. I know a young woman who lost her husband to cancer several years ago. And although she was able to relinquish him into God's hands, it was more difficult to relinquish herself to God. She wanted to rush out of the loss and into a new life because watching her husband die had been such a long and painful process. She felt she had already grieved for him throughout the months of his dying. Looking back, she is most grateful to God, not for comforting her in grief, but for teaching her how to live in her grief. For it was in grieving and in waiting on God that she found his blessing and his presence.

Only when we feel abandoned by the world or by those we

love are we at a touch point with God where we can truly abandon ourselves to him. This relinquishment of our souls, this casting off and emptying of ourselves, leads us to a place where we are ready to receive God's grace.

Receive. In one late-night conversation and confession, I watched my eighteen-year marriage crumble at my feet. Devastated by the loss, a desert river flowed from my torrent of tears. But for the first time in a long time, I also knew I was in the best position to receive God's tender love and blessing through his strength, his word and his people, and I did not take them lightly or push them away. I opened my life to fully receive his mercy as I called on friends when I needed to talk or work through fears. Cards and letters of encouragement felt like opening physical symbols of God's blessings, anointing me with the oil of his Spirit as I read them over and over. Through this painful humbling of my heart, God has lifted me up to receive these good and perfect gifts. Only when I am empty am I able to receive his fullness. Therein I find that all I can do is worship him in increasing measure.

Worship. It surprises me when I go back and read my journals from my desert time. While my heart experienced dryness, brokenness and, at times, even numbness, God's Spirit ministered to my spirit through remembrances of his promises and his power. Day by day I recorded and clung to his Word as he affirmed his path of renewal: "He who began a good work in me is faithful to complete it . . . Fear not . . . I will never leave you or forsake you . . . Trust in the Lord . . . Lean not on your own understanding . . . My soul waits on the Lord." As I meditate on the words from God's heart, it invariably leads me to praise and worship him. I acknowledge his perfect wisdom, power and glory; I adore his holiness and majesty, his justice and mercy; and the more I worship, the more my troubled heart is soothed and the more the strife subsides.

Thinking back, I see the paradox that learning to wait calls me to worship. For when I least feel like praying and worshiping is when I most need to do so as an act of obedience, of submitting my heart to God rather than bowing to the troubles of the day. When I submit, he leads me to a higher rock for a more perfect perspective. And as I walk with him, he continually draws me to hidden refreshment in the weary land where I can drink in the water of life.

REST STOP

What is the most difficult part of waiting on God for you? To relinquish, to receive or to worship? Likely the one that is most difficult is the one most needed during your time of waiting.

- In the end I find that waiting is not about wishing away the difficulties of life. It is about climbing to higher ground with God.

- Waiting is not about feeling bored with God and doing something to make the wait tolerable in the meantime. It is about finding God in the ruts and routines and staying close to his side.

- Waiting is not about soaring on spiritual or emotional highs. It is about planting roots to keep me anchored in the storms.

- And waiting is not about hoping for a problem-free life. It is about living an abundant life with a heart fully devoted to God alone.

Change and loss are inevitable, but beneath the surface of external change hides the inner mystery of new beginnings and renewed life, if we're willing to wait.

A DESERT JOURNEY

Read Luke 2:25-35, and meditate on this scene in your imagination:

If they'd heard it once, they'd heard it a million times. "One day we'll see with our own eyes, the Consolation of Israel, God's very own Messiah! Just wait, you'll see." But Simeon's wife, his children and their own families wondered, "When?" The presence of Roman political power weighed heavily in their lives. First, there was the ridiculous census that disrupted everyone's life by requiring that they all return to their place of birth. Then, the new tax would come as a result of the census. And always, the visible signs of power loomed, mocking the Israelites' freedom and God's sovereign rule in their lives. Centurions roamed the streets, and politicians and troops occupied buildings and even places of worship.

"If ever there were a time for Israel to be consoled, now is the time." Simeon nodded and smiled as his wife mumbled her complaints to God about the noisy soldiers just outside. He finished tying his sandals and reached for his walking stick, ready to go to the temple for morning prayers. But something stopped him. Stunned by the presence of God's Spirit in him and in his city, he covered his face with his hands and wept. Immediately his wife ran to him and fell at his feet. "What is it, Simeon? What's wrong?" She had been worried about her husband for weeks. So often he spoke about leaving this world in peace, after he had seen the Promised One for himself. She wondered if he'd had a premonition about his own death. And so she watched his every move. Was it time?

Simeon lifted his head, his eyes wide with wonder. "Today's the day," he whispered. And he rose from his seat with renewed strength, hugged his wife and hurried as fast as his hobbled bones would take him into the streets and to-

ward the temple. Others made their way to worship as well. Simeon always stopped and acknowledged in his spirit the commotion of the moneychangers, animals and people from all walks of life. The temple was the epitome of the world colliding headlong into holiness, sending lives into a ruckus of change and loss, sacrifice and offerings. But today he didn't stop for long.

"How will I know?" Simeon prayed aloud. He climbed the steps toward the temple, certain of his leading. He entered the quieter, muted sounds of the inner courtyard, searching, waiting, watching. And as he waited, he was struck by another vision. It disturbed and changed him all at once as his expectation of the Redeemer was consumed by the light of God's truth and glory. For the Consolation came not in peace and freedom but through a tearing and ripping of cloth, and behind the veil he saw the redemption and consolation pouring forth like brilliant light, not just for Israel but for the Gentiles as well, for all the world.

As a sword of truth pierced souls, the maimed, the sick and the heartbroken entered through the tear behind the veil, as if invited straight into the Holy of Holies. And as they entered, they were changed. Lives rising and falling all entered into the brilliance and were clothed in righteousness.

The holy vision sent Simeon to his knees, his face to the floor. He saw in the end the glory of God with arms stretched out to receive humanity. Drawn by the light, Simeon himself entered in and saw not the mighty warrior he had assumed would redeem his people. Rather, that great light poured from a baby's wooden cradle. And the cry of an infant intruded into his vision as slowly it faded away. And then he knew.

He raised his eyes and met the poorest of poor families and heard the very real cry of the baby from his vision, held in the arms of a woman who appeared to have seen the light as well. Simeon's eyes met the child's, and at last he beheld his Messiah. Wonder and joy, praise and honor poured from the depth of his soul.

All he could do, all he wanted to do, was hold his Salvation. And he reached toward the child. The child's mother smiled and handed the Son of God to the elder of Israel as he prayed aloud, "Sovereign Lord, as you have *promised, you now dismiss your servant in peace. For my eyes have seen your salvation that you have prepared in the sight of all people, a light for revelation to the Gentiles and for glory to your people Israel." His wait was over.*

HIDDEN JOY

- What image of Christ has given you the greatest consolation in the past? Is it the Good Shepherd, the Living Word, the Bread of Heaven, the Vine, the Great Physician, the Prince of Peace, the King of Kings or the Light of the World? Or has God given a special image just to you? What does that special vision mean to you, and when did it become meaningful?

- When have you waited for God in your spiritual journey? Is there something that you are waiting for now? Describe what it was like when God finally arrived or made his presence known to you. Did the waiting change you in either a positive or negative way?

- Read Habakkuk 1:1-3 and 3:17-19. Consider the changes that Habakkuk must have longed for as he waited for God's deliverance of his people. How did he relinquish, receive and worship? How did it help him wait on the Lord?

- Read Acts 9:1-19 about Saul's (Paul's) conversion. What kind of changes did Paul deal with? Why do you think God blinded him for three days? Meditate on what those three days may have been like for Saul. What did he do during that time? What do the images of light and darkness reveal to you about waiting?

6

INTIMACY . . .

in the Desert of Loneliness

*God is the Creator and the protector and the lover. For until
I am substantially united to him, I can never have perfect rest
or true happiness, until, that is, I am so attached to him that
there can be no created thing between my God and me.*

JULIAN OF NORWICH, SHOWINGS

QUIET YOUR HEART

Read Ezekiel 16:1-14. Meditate on this graphic picture of loneliness in the words
"thrown out . . . despised . . . naked and bare." Now overlay those words with
God's grace as he speaks, "Live . . . I spread the corner of my garment over you . . .
you became mine . . . bathes you . . . clothed you . . . covered you . . . so you were
adorned." Let these intimate words touch your heart.

ENTER HIS PRESENCE

Read Psalm 34:1-10. Consider how those who love God want for nothing more
and "lack no good thing." Make this your prayer today.

By nature I'm an introvert. I have an affinity with solitude and silence. But as comfortable as I am with being alone, I still experience bouts of loneliness. It arrives at nearly every stage of life:

- Observe a child on the first day of school, and you'll see the first pangs of a lonely heart.

- Watch an adolescent attempting to bridge the span between childhood and adulthood, and you'll see the lonely ache that coming of age brings.

- Look into the eyes of a father walking his daughter down a long church aisle, and you'll see the loneliness found in an empty nest.

- Consider a respected CEO put on a pedestal above all other co-workers, and you'll see the loneliness in longing to just come down and be one of the crowd.

- Sit in a funeral home with a widow, and you'll physically ache from the weight of a lonely existence without a lifelong mate.

Sometimes that longing called loneliness is for a particular person, sometimes for any person and sometimes just for a place to belong. It is a homesickness that leaves us weepy. But as I contemplate what loneliness is, I am aware that these feelings can strip me of my sense of identity as I stand shivering and vulnerable before the world, and even before God who sees everything "uncovered and laid bare" (Hebrews 4:13). I may begin to doubt myself and whether I am valued by others. It is this value vacuum that draws me to want to connect to someone or something in a more intimate way.

But these seasons of loneliness have also become the defining moments of my faith as I've turned inward and examined my own heart and turned Godward to see that even though I stand bare and shivering, he comes to me in great tenderness to quell the pain of my barren heart.

EMBRACING LONELINESS

Loneliness defines a longing, yearning or desire for deep and meaningful connections. All these longings fall within the bounds of God's indelible image stamped on our souls. Even before sin entered paradise, Adam searched for someone like himself. Loneliness is not sin; nor is it a disease to be avoided. Rather, it is a sign, maybe even an alarm, to turn our hearts to God, who reveals his deep love for us through our deep longings for intimacy. "Our hearts are restless until they find rest in you."[1]

So why is it never simple to deal with loneliness? Because it feels uncomfortable. We don't like to be alone; we don't like silence, and few are willing to stop and listen to it. Loneliness traps us like quicksand. For the harder we try to avoid it, the more mired we become in it.

As I have traveled my own paths of loneliness, I've noticed that my first reaction is to escape it by taking a detour from

God's direction as I try to quench my own thirst for connection. I have plunged into groups of people to avoid being alone. And I have searched for intimate relationships with individuals I barely knew. But as much as I wanted these drastic measures to bolster my lonely heart, they only increased my thirst. In these make-believe relationships, where I pretended that everything was fine, a lonely ache remained deep inside. When humanity fails to satisfy, my reaction is to withdraw within myself and disconnect further from the pain of empty relationships. But this only compacts the loneliness into a more concentrated form.

We fill our lives with shallow relationships, noise and unceasing conversation, trying to free ourselves from the grip of this desert place, never realizing that only when we relax in God's arms, listen to his voice and love his presence can he use our loneliness to strengthen our walk with him. My responsibility in the midst of loneliness is simply to become teachable and willing to learn these lessons as I travel on this path through the desert.

Emptiness becomes the first step toward wholeness. Loneliness is a path toward knowing myself and knowing God. When I refuse the lie whispering in the dark, "You're incomplete without someone else," I embrace the truth that in Christ I am whole. But that realization doesn't always arrive in a neat little package. I have traveled down a road littered with loss and longing. Shortly after my separation from my husband, my journal entry read:

> Lord, I don't even know what the next step is, except to look at you, to listen for your voice, to trust you. Without warning, pain and sadness and loss, rather than being a great emptiness that

leaves me speechless, now well up in me, sweep over me and fill every pore so completely that great sobs wrack my body and tears pour out, draining away the pain to give me a tiny pocket of air to breathe so that I don't drown in the sorrow. I realize not how empty I am, but how full of pain. But I also sense that I'm being poured out, emptied by you, so that I can have more of you. A paradox: What the world sees as emptiness and lone-liness is truly an overwhelming fullness, a yearning that begs to be released. And only when I release it am I in a position to be fully completed by you.

It's a fact. "There are two easy ways to die in the desert: thirst or drowning. . . . This place is stained with such ironies, a ten-sion set between the need to find water and the need to get away from it. The floods that come with the least warning ar-rive at the hottest time of the year."[2] In seasons of loneliness, emotion can sweep in like a flashflood in the desert. One minute we're thirsty for connection, the next we're drowning in pain. God uses these faith-stretching, heart-breaking times to make me "mature and complete, not lacking anything" (James 1:4).

As I encounter other seasons of loneliness, depression or disappointment, I need to be reminded of the truth that full-ness comes out of experiences of emptiness. I am thankful that as I walk through those barren times that inevitably come, God reassures me that I have been "filled to the measure of all the fullness of God" (Ephesians 3:19). There I see him close at hand, teaching me and filling me with his presence.

Life's greatest challenges must be faced alone with God. In those tough times that define who we are and what we're all about, we must go alone into the depths of God. Even with the best human love and support, deep down we know that paths of hardship must be walked alone, clinging only to the God of all comfort for direction. Author Gerhard Frost wrote, "Life's journey is single file. As Martin Luther said, 'Everyone has to do his own believing, just as everyone has to do his own dying.' . . . Sooner or later, one stands before the Lord. Not with parents, family, friends, or humanity in general—all alone, alone with the big questions—this is my life situation and yours."[3]

Jesus faced this hardship one night as he entered the Garden of Gethsemane for the struggle of his life. It seems being alone was the last thing Christ wanted, because he asked three friends to go with him through this emotional and spiritual battle. They went, but fell asleep on the job. So, like most of us, Jesus grappled with God and with his own will alone. One of the hardest aspects of loneliness is the awareness that no one can accompany us on a difficult path that God paves for us alone. But on that path we walk in friendship with God.

In fourteenth-century medieval England, a woman known as Dame Julian took on the ancient vocation of anchoress in Norwich. As an anchoress, Julian was cloistered in a small room within the church, withdrawn from society in order to completely devote herself to prayer, contemplation and spiritual direction for those who sought her counsel. She lived there for decades until her death in the early fifteenth century. In this lonely profession, Julian's understanding of God's love and goodness blossomed. In her solitude she wrote, "God, of your goodness, give me yourself, for you are enough for me and I can ask for nothing . . . less which can pay you full worship. And if I ask for anything . . . less always I am in want; but only in you do I have everything."[4]

Practicing the spiritual discipline of solitude is crucial in the life of a Christian because it builds us up to face those lonely trials that inevitably befall us all. When we cultivate solitude in times of plenty, we harvest its peace in times of loneliness. Learning to strip away the distractions and focus solely on God trains us to hear his voice and find our bearings on our journey through life.

REST STOP

Read the following passages, and note the ways that God fills you up when you are empty and the ways he walks with you when you are alone: Psalm 36:7-10; 63:1-8.

RIVERS OF DELIGHT

Loneliness is a force that can lead us to God and that allows us to travel with him on the road toward intimacy.

Loneliness leads me to God's companionship. It impels me to partner with others. "Praise be to . . . God . . . the Father of compassion and the God of all comfort, who comforts us in all our troubles, so that we can comfort those in any trouble with the comfort we ourselves have received from God" (2 Corinthians 1:3-4). The word *comfort* literally means to come alongside of someone. When loneliness rises up in me, I feel almost embarrassed or self-conscious that I am by myself. Those insecure feelings that devalue my sense of purpose hinder my ability to reach out to others and thus perpetuate the loneliness into a downward spiral that leaves little room for anyone else.

But from that point of loneliness, Christ reaches down to lift me up. From the beginning of Genesis through the end of Revelation, we meet a God who walks with us. And the best picture of God walking with me is seen in Jesus, the offspring of God come to earth, conceived in woman, born through blood and water, who hammered nails, sawed wood and traipsed through dusty desert paths in Israel. He is Emmanuel, God *with* us. That is different than God *for* us. It is the message that the shepherds heard: A Savior has been born *to you*!

In the lonely wilderness, God comes to us and walks with us as a companion through our trials.

> When you pass through the rivers,
>   they will not sweep over you.
> When you walk through the fire,
>   you will not be burned. (Isaiah 43:2)

The Gospel is always about God coming, God reaching, God drawing, God equipping, God saving. And that is why it is such good news. I don't have to worry about whether or not I'm doing the right thing in the right way with enough sincerity and frequency to get God to pay attention. It is because of our loneliness and homesickness for him that he initiated this relationship with us. We can trust him to never leave us alone. He could have chosen to leave us outside of Eden's gates long ago, cast out and destroyed. But over and over again, he reaches to me and you in the most outlandish ways.

He invites us to deepen our intimate relationship with him when he calls us to "'come!' . . . Whoever is thirsty, let him come; and whoever wishes, let him take the free gift of the water of life" (Revelation 22:17). He is the gracious host, and he longs for us to accept his invitation to dwell with him, to be at home with him and to dine with him.

Loneliness leads me to God's table. One of the loneliest feelings is sitting at a table by myself in the middle of a busy restaurant. Where do I put my eyes? What do I do with my hands? Is anyone wondering if there is something wrong with me, or am I just so absorbed in myself that I assume someone might have a thought toward me when, in fact, I am not even noticed?

But there is one in the desert who has set a place just for me. He escorts me to his banquet table, "and his banner over me is love" (Song of Songs 2:4). This banner is a canopy like the one used in the Jewish wedding ceremonies where the bride and groom express their covenant of love. There we delight in our mutual companionship and dine on the pleasures of love. "I delight to sit in his shade, and his fruit is sweet to my taste" (Song of Songs 2:3). This is the fruit of the vine that comes from abiding in him. He is the vine; I am the branch, and he strengthens me with the wine of the fruit, the symbol of the blood he gave for me. His table is spread out as an act of loving sacrifice. Bread and wine: his own body and blood.

I have often grappled with the difficult passage of Scripture found in the Gospel of John. It is easy to understand the symbolic verse in 6:35 where Jesus says, "I am the bread of life." But he doesn't stop there. He continues and says, "My flesh is real food and my blood is real drink. Whoever eats my flesh and drinks my blood remains in me, and I in him" (John 6:55-56). This is a complete acceptance and partaking of his sacrifice that ministers to our hearts daily. I must realize that Christ's physical body was fully given over to me so that my spirit can attain complete redemption. Feeding every day on that sacrifice, gazing at the crucified Christ, brings me to a place of peace and pardon and opens a new realm of intimacy between us.

But it is at this complete integration of Christ's body into our spirit and Christ's Spirit into our body where many followers fail to come with everything they have and exchange it for everything Christ has. And thus they turn and leave his side. But a few, like Peter, remain and accept the body and the blood and proclaim, "To whom shall we go?" (John 6:68). We have no one else in heaven or on earth who can wholly satisfy our thirsty souls. And I cry out, "Where else can I take my lonely heart? Whom have I in heaven or on earth who will satisfy my deepest longing for connection and love?"

Loneliness leads me to the fellowship of believers. There is nothing worse than feeling lonely in a group of people, feeling ignored, different, like a stranger. But from the dawn of time until today, God created us to be in relationship with others. He told Adam in the garden, "It is not good for the man to be alone" (Genesis 2:18). The psalmist wrote, "God sets the lonely in families" (Psalm 68:6). And in the New Testament we see Jesus call a small group of followers to be his close friends. He could have fulfilled his purpose alone without company, but as a human, he too longed for the connection of intimate friends.

Being joined with a community of believers doesn't just happen by some miracle. It requires effort and a commitment of time on our part to make connections. It means feeling a bit uncomfortable until I am fully connected to even one person, let alone an entire congregation. But the more I have been willing to use my spiritual gifts, to offer hospitality first and to see others through God's eyes, the sooner I have made those connections.

REST STOP

Read Hebrews 10:24-25. How has being together with other believers spurred you on in your faith? How have you encouraged someone else's faith?

Although there is no quick cure for lonesome feelings, by being open to God's care we can begin to understand his willingness to teach us his ways in the wilderness. Julian heard words of comfort early in her life when God's Spirit spoke such assurances to her: "And so our good Lord answered to all the questions and doubts which I could raise, saying most comfortingly: I may make all things well, and I can make all things well; and I shall make all things well; and I will make all things well; and you will see yourself that every kind of thing will be well. . . . And in these . . . words God wishes us to be enclosed in rest and in peace."[5]

Armed with God's intimate comfort, the barren desert of loneliness no longer sends me into a panic, looking for an escape route. Instead, I recognize it as a season that comes to all humans, a path we all travel, a tool in God's hands that is able to enrich us, help us grow and fill our deepest need. Loneliness calls me to cling to God. Loneliness pulls me to walk with God. Loneliness empties me to allow room for God. Loneliness opens me to embrace others in God.

A DESERT JOURNEY

Read Luke 10:30-35, and picture this scene in your mind:

As much as he knew the dangers, he also knew he had to go. He had to reach Jericho to see his dying father before death beat him to it. Usually people traveled in groups of three or more as protection against the bands of rob-

bers who took advantage of poor souls who appeared to be easy targets. There was no time today to find traveling companions. He had to leave on his own. He carried a walking stick as a weapon, praying he wouldn't need it, and tied a small moneybag around his waist, hidden under his robe.

He walked steadily most of the day and began to hope that he would make it safely to his father's bedside by late afternoon. A scuffle from behind startled him. Before he could turn to see, two men shoved him hard to the ground, grabbed his walking stick and began to beat him with it until he slipped into unconsciousness. He didn't know how much time had passed, but when he awoke, the sun was beginning to set. His head throbbed, and he felt a gash above his eye, which was swollen shut. They had torn away his robe, and he knew, even before he touched his side, that the pouch of coins would be gone. Never had he felt so alone and frightened.

Over the next several minutes, he crawled closer to the path, hoping help would arrive before darkness fell. When he saw someone approaching, he recognized him as a priest. "Mercy," he called out. But the priest quickly looked away and hurried to the opposite side of the road, never looking back. The injured man felt lightheaded. Pebbles and dry plant life made it impossible to lie comfortably. Soon more footsteps. He prayed it was not another robber and called out feebly, "Mercy." He lifted his head slightly and held out his hand, but this traveler, a Levite, also walked as far away from the man as possible.

Finally a poor man with a donkey came upon the injured man who had no strength even to call to him. "Sir, let me help," the traveler whispered as he knelt at his side. Quickly he brought water and let him drink. He pulled a jar of oil and wine from a bag slung over the donkey's back and poured the mixture over the man's wounds. He tore his own cloak to provide strips of cloth to bind the wounds and finally helped the man to his feet. "You ride," he simply instructed as he lifted him to the donkey's back.

He didn't remember the rest of the journey, but he awoke in the morning clean, cared for and with a bowl of hot broth next to his bed. The fear lifted. He heard the stranger who had helped him speaking to the innkeeper, "Take these silver coins and look after him. I'll return and pay for any extra charges *you may have." Before he could offer his thanks, the stranger was gone, but the promise of his return filled him with hope and he knew that all would be well.*

HIDDEN JOY

- What aspects of loneliness do you think the injured man experienced? How can the attitudes of the priest, the Levite and the injured man be compared to people in today's society?

- Although this parable Jesus told illustrates how we are to love our neighbor, how can the Samaritan symbolize the way Jesus comes to us and loves us in our time of loneliness? Has loneliness ever felt like a wound to you? In what ways?

- How does the way the Samaritan took the man to an inn to provide for him reveal how Christ connects us to other people?

- Read the story of Hagar in Genesis 16. What reasons did Hagar have for feeling a sense of loneliness? What can you learn about God from his conversation with Hagar in the desert?

- Read Daniel 6. How is this story about standing strong in the faith a picture of living with loneliness? How did Daniel experience God's presence even in the midst of loneliness? What practical steps can you take to connect with God as Daniel did?

7

VICTORY . . .

in the Desert of Trials

*We are not meant to shake with fear when faced by temptations.
We may look up to Him who conquered the powers of evil. . . .
Those powers can never say that He did not conquer them, for
He both exposed them and made a show of conquering them
openly. Therefore, we follow in procession behind a triumphant
Christ! And if all our reliance is placed upon Him, we need
never be defeated in spirit. Today, from hour to hour, He can and
will lead us on to triumph—if we look to Him.*

AMY CARMICHAEL, *EDGES OF HIS WAY*

QUIET YOUR HEART

Read Isaiah 30:20. Adversity and affliction are described here as "bread and water," a meal given to prisoners. Yet, even in such meager conditions, God points
the way and says you will see your teachers and hear encouragement whispered
in your ear. Consider how God is reaching you in the midst of trials. Even though
they often feel overwhelming, can you see small signs of God's provision during
these trials? If you cannot hear him whispering encouragement just now, what
would you like to hear him say? Express this desire to God in prayer.

ENTER HIS PRESENCE

Read Isaiah 40:28-31 several times. Then close your eyes and picture God as the ea-
gle soaring on the breezes far above your troubled world. See him catch you on his
own wings as you soar with him without even an ounce of effort on your part. Sense
your strength returning and your power increasing. Thank him for his enabling love.

I DECIDED LONG AGO THAT THE HARDEST TESTS OF MY faith do not lie in the big challenges of life but in the tiny temptations. It is just that the ordinary stuff gets overlooked as "no big deal." Yet these everyday failures can keep us off balance, unable to move forward in our walk with Christ. Why, if we claim victory in Jesus, do so many Christians appear defeated, unable to grow up spiritually or overcome addictive sin? They seem to do more harm than good to the kingdom of God. Truth be told, I have been one of those Christians, and I have the potential to be one on any given day at any given hour.

Two women came to my door recently to leave their denominational magazine and to find out if we were Christians. My teenage daughter politely chatted with the women, told them she was a Christian, took their literature and thanked them for stopping. A week later they returned to follow up with her, to see if she had read the material and wanted to talk further. Uncomfortable with their theology, I went to the door and told these women in a most terse voice, "We're Christians, and we don't need your magazines," and I quickly closed the door before they could even speak, self-satisfied that I had snatched my child from the clutches of some cult.

It didn't take long for the Holy Spirit to convict me of my brutal and arrogant words. I was aghast, as was my daughter, at my behavior. How could someone so in love with Jesus suddenly explode in judgmental, self-righteous behavior? No doubt my witness had done more harm than good to everyone involved.

I confessed my sin to God and asked my daughter to forgive my behavior. We discussed what had happened, what I'd done wrong, how I could have handled it better and how those women seemed to have a more compassionate witness than I had. Yet following our conversation, I had a tremendous sense of thankfulness that when defeat knocked me down, God picked me back up. "We are hard pressed on every side, but not crushed; perplexed, but not in despair, persecuted, but not abandoned; struck down, but not destroyed" (2 Corinthians 4:7-9). I had failed God in that moment, but immediately I thirsted for his victory poured out in his mercy over my sinful heart. I continue to pray that God will allow me to see others with his eyes, to love others with his heart and that my own weak nature will never bar the way for his mercy to flow through me.

REST STOP

Contemplate ways you may have failed God or discredited his name. Have you confessed that failure to him? Ask him to take it from you and use it as a tool to teach you his ways. Now claim his victory over your failure and praise his name.

EMBRACING VICTORY

Victory is an old-fashioned word that I need to reclaim in my desert journey where I often feel defeated by trials or temptation. There are choices I can make that will keep me firmly on the path in my pilgrimage with Christ. These are the choices Christ himself made as he was tested, not only in the wilderness but also throughout his life on earth.

Choose to give God unlimited access to our heart. This is what David frequently did as he prayed one of the most difficult prayers to pray:

> Search me, O God, and know my heart. . . .
> See if there is any offensive way in me. (Psalm 139:23-24)

Failure to give God access, to yield to the examination of his Spirit, stunts our growth. If we confine God only to the areas of life where we are comfortable letting him in and shut him out of those places that most need his touch, then victory lies dormant in the fallow fields of our souls. This is what the Israelites did in the wilderness.

> How often they rebelled against him in the desert
>   and grieved him in the wasteland!
> Again and again they put God to the test;
>   they vexed the Holy One of Israel.
> They did not remember his power. (Psalm 78:40-41)

The King James Version interprets *vexed* as "they limited God." But Jesus said in the midst of his own wilderness, "Do not put the Lord your God to the test" (Luke 4:12). In other words, don't vex God or limit him in any way. When I limit God by refusing his Spirit and ignoring his power at work in me, then I forfeit his gifts of grace.

> If only you had paid attention to my commands,
>   your peace would have been like a river. (Isaiah 48:18)

In the end, I am the one who loses out when I turn God into a would-have-been God.

While he possesses all power and has all ability to *make* us obedient, he instilled within each of us a gift of free will to accept or reject him. It takes mutual agreement between each of us and God to allow his glory to shine forth. "Will we let God be as he is, majestic and holy, vast and wondrous, or will we always be trying to whittle him down to the size of our small minds, insist on confining him within the boundaries we are comfortable with, refuse to think of him other than in images that are convenient to our lifestyle?"[1]

Choose to thirst for God above all others. Jesus, during his forty-day wilderness trial said, "Worship the Lord your God and serve *him only*" (Luke 4:8, emphasis added). Often we assume that when we find God and receive his living water, we will be satisfied once and for all and can go about our life the way we want. We receive the cup of salvation, but rarely return to splash in the streams of living water that flow from within us (John 7:38). "Everything is made to center upon the initial act of 'accepting Christ' . . . and we are not expected thereafter to crave any further revelation of God to our souls. We have been snared in the coils of a spurious logic which insists that if we have found Him, we need no more seek Him."[2] The reason Jesus told the woman at the well that she would never thirst again is not because her thirst would disappear but because the water would never run dry (John 4).

Victory does not occur when we finally lose our thirst, but when we gain it. Jesus cried out on the cross, "I thirst." Physically he was dehydrated, exhausted. Spiritually he thirsted for God in a way he never had before, for he could no longer sense

God close at hand. He had a choice, just as we do. He could have chosen to turn his back on God and on all humanity and follow his own will to fight against the torture. But instead he turned toward God and thirsted for him above all others. He placed his life into God's hands and cried a simple prayer of victory that said, "I thirst." Rather than complaining about my thirst for God, perhaps I should be asking, "Is my thirst deep enough?" Oh, that I would thirst for you more, Lord.

Choose to love God's Word. Feed on it. "Man does not live on bread alone, but on every word that comes from the mouth of God" (Matthew 4:4). Those Christian men and women down through the centuries whose words continue to inspire and challenge us today are those who continuously fed on and were nourished by the Word of God. His Word is our armor, equipping us with faith, truth, righteousness and readiness. The Word is God-breathed. It literally contains his Spirit, his breath of life. And we are in constant and desperate need of spiritual resuscitation.

Here is where our thirst for God is not just quenched but instilled. And when we thirst for God, he provides unceasing drink. "If we have a godly thirst, it will appear by diligence in frequenting the place and means of grace; brute beasts for want of water will break through hedges, and grace-thirsty souls will make their ways through all encumbrances to come where they may have satisfaction."[3]

REST STOP

Consider these three choices as you face trials and temptations. Which one, if any, do you feel you consistently choose in God's favor? Which one do you need to work on? Read Isaiah 41:17-20 as a means of visualizing God's pleasure as you choose to follow him.

RIVERS OF DELIGHT

Victory in Christ is perhaps the greatest of all God's mysteries, for it is in suffering, death and loss where victory is gained. There is no victory unless a battle is waged. There is no one who overcomes unless obstacles are hurdled. We want the victory, but few are willing to wage the fight. We want Easter joy without Good Friday sorrow. We want Christmas cheer without the dark, damp manger. We want the Good Shepherd but not the wounded Lamb of God. If I only want something to make me feel good for a time, then I am not thirsty enough for God.

Amy Carmichael, a missionary in India for most of her life, founded a home for children in the early 1900s. Known for her deep devotion to Christ, her work touched thousands of lives and affected Indian culture through her effort to outlaw temple prostitution, where boys and girls were being sold into bondage. Midway through Amy's life, a freak accident left her bedridden. There she lived her final years in constant and often unbearable pain. Many wondered why such a devoted servant of God would be taken from active work. But it was through the veil of pain and suffering that Amy discovered the depths of God's love, and that legacy is best seen in these hard places of victory.

Victory in suffering: "We are . . . co-heirs with Christ, if indeed we share in his sufferings in order that we may also share in his glory" (Romans 8:17). To find victory we must expect the pain and loss resulting from battle. Amy wondered why Christians are so surprised by the pain of life, and she expressed these thoughts as if Christ himself were asking her:

Hast thou no scar?
No hidden scar on foot, or side or hands?
I hear thee sung as mighty in the land,

I hear them hail thy bright ascendant star,
Hast thou no scar?
Hast thou no wound?
Yet I was wounded by the archers, spent,
Leaned Me against a tree to die; and rent
By ravening beasts that compassed Me, I swooned:
Hast *thou* no wound?
No wound? No scar?
Yet, as the Master shall the servant be,
And pierced are the feet that follow Me;
But thine are whole: can he have followed far
Who has no wound nor scar?[4]

As a follower of Jesus, it is a given that I will have scars. If my goal for spiritual maturity is conformity to Christ (Romans 8:29), then how can I expect to live a life absent from pain and spiritual warfare? "For our struggle is not against flesh and blood, but against the rulers, against the authorities, against the powers of this dark world and against the spiritual forces of evil in the heavenly realms" (Ephesians 6:12).

Victory in death. When living in pain, with death knocking at the door, those who spend their time contemplating the cross of Jesus receive relief and understanding. Amy Carmichael was no exception. In the shadow of the cross, she shared Christ's suffering as a privilege and learned what it truly meant to die to self, to take up her cross and follow Jesus. "I have been crucified with Christ and I no longer live, but Christ lives in me" (Galatians 2:20).

This was not just a high, spiritual concept but rather a down-to-earth reality that broke into her everyday world. In ordinary choices, she often considered putting her own desires aside as "a chance to die" for Christ. When anger flared from an unkind word, she prayed for "a chance to die," and therein found her victory. Perhaps her best-loved work, titled "If," considers how self-centered behavior convicts the heart that "I know nothing of Calvary's love."

> If I hold on to choices of any kind, just because they are my choices . . .
> if I give more room to my private likes and dislikes . . .
> if I am soft on myself and slide easily and comfortably into the vice of self-pity and eliciting sympathy . . .
> if, the very moment I am conscious of the shadow of "self" crossing that inner threshold, I do not shut the door and (in the power of Him who works in us to will and to do) keep that door shut . . .
> then I know nothing of Calvary's love.[5]

Victory in failure. "But whatever was to my profit I now consider loss for the sake of Christ" (Philippians 3:7). More than once, Peter failed to follow Jesus. When he claimed he would never forsake him, he denied him three times. When he took a step of faith to walk on water, he sank. But in the denying and sinking, he always returned to and reached for Jesus, realizing there was no better place to be than at the Lord's side.

Amy Carmichael expressed victory in failure like this: "He who begins, finishes. He who leads us on, follows behind to deal in love with our poor attempts. . . . He gathers up the things that we have dropped—fallen resolutions, our mistakes. . . . He makes His blessed pardon to flow over our sins till they are utterly washed away. And He turns to fight the Enemy, who would pursue after us, to destroy us from behind. *He is first, and He is last!* And we are gathered up in between, as in great arms of eternal lovingkindness."[6]

REST STOP

Read Philippians 3:7-11. How does Paul address the victory in suffering, death and failure in this passage? What does victory in Christ look like to you?

Victory requires faith. Victory requires a Mighty God. Victory requires a union of the two: Faith in a Mighty God. And faith begins with our confidence in God's character. We know God more deeply as we learn to revere him and humble ourselves at the cross of Christ.

REVERE GOD

Victory releases my weakness and self-consciousness and embraces God more. I move from my guilt to God's mercy, from my shame to God's glory, from my lack to God's abundance. The victory of faith that overcomes the world acknowledges my confidence in God's character. As I practice reverence, I increase my level of God-confidence through worship.

Scripture often uses the phrase "fear the Lord" as an act of worship. Still, we shy away from such language today because we want a user-friendly God. But the fear of the Lord involves a deep respect and intimate trust. Psalm 25:14 says, "The LORD confides in those who fear him." I love to think of myself as God's confidant just as he is mine. Like a most intimate friend, when I fear God, he reveals his secret longings and purposes to me.

> I will give you the treasures of darkness,
>> riches stored in secret places,
> so that you may know that I am the LORD. (Isaiah 45:3)

The list of his attributes and magnificent character is endless. But consider how strong our faith becomes when we meditate on these truths:

- God is almighty—he raises up nations but knows when a single sparrow falls.

- God is all-wise—he is capable, skilled, righteous and just, and he sees me in light of eternity.

- God is all-love—He seeks me, delights in me, disciplines me and loves me even before I loved him.

REST STOP

Read Psalm 96. In your journal list other characteristics of God reflected in this psalm and what they mean to you personally. Spend a few minutes praising him for who he is and asking him for the desire to know him more intimately through worship.

CLING TO THE CROSS

Perseverance in victory requires that I cling to the cross when defeat comes again and again. I have considered how Jesus was tempted and suffered like me in every way. But I struggle with the thought that although he was tempted, he never gave in to it—never sinned. He never dealt with a guilty conscience or the mortified guilt of repeated offense to God. He was never caught in the cycle of addiction or the confusion and consequences of poor personal choices.

But if I follow Jesus all the way to the cross and listen to his
words, I cannot deny that he knew, in a way much deeper than
I will ever know, the weight of sin. He held not just the guilt of
one life, as you and I have, but the guilt of the whole world. I
don't believe he went to the cross blind to the specifics of each
sin he bore. In his omniscience he saw the individual sins of the
world, past, present and future. He took as his own the vilest,
most profane, morbid and grotesque sins. He bore each deceitful, sneaky, secret sin. He grasped the horrific, the idolatrous
and the self-centered sins. As a member of the human race,
born into sin, he experienced the life-destroying pain of guilt.
And yet, in the extremes of pain, suffering and death, he received God's forgiveness and poured it out on his tormentors.
He tended to his broken-hearted mother and best friend. And
he worshiped God as he put his final breath into his Father's
hands.

In this picture of unabashed humility and suffering, he tri-
umphed for us all.

> Therefore God exalted him to the highest place
>   and gave him the name that is above every name,
> that at the name of Jesus every knee should bow . . .
> and every tongue confess that Jesus Christ is Lord,
>   to the glory of God the Father. (Philippians 2:9-11)

I have decided that life will always challenge me, but the
challenges, and even failure, cannot defeat me. In fact, God's
Word reassures me over and over that nothing can separate me
from his love. Nothing. No trouble, hardship, persecution,
famine, nakedness, danger or sword. Not death or life, not angels or demons, not the present nor the future, nor any power
that towers high above me or reaches deeper than hell. Noth-

ing in all creation can break the bond of love between me and my God (Romans 8:35 paraphrased).

- Victory does not necessarily mean that the battle is over or the desert a distant memory.

- Victory lies in overcoming my petty attitude that demands life be fair, that proclaims it is my right, that shoves others aside to be first and best.

- Victory is the ability to "get over myself" and lift others up.

- Victory lies in taking a towel and stooping to wipe the feet of the poor, the strange and the hungry.

- Victory lies in singing and dancing in the midst of trouble, knowing God is at work creating something new out of the old and the pain.

For in the midst of suffering and loss, temptation and trials, I run to the cross of my Savior and see the one who suffered and died for me, the one who has been tested and tempted like me. And we are forever bound and wrapped together in the intimacy of shared pain and ultimate victory.

THE DESERT JOURNEY

Read Mark 10:17-31, and picture this scene in your imagination:

He pulled on his finest robe, which was made from woven silk, trimmed with gold. His breakfast had been prepared and set by the servants of the house. He nodded his thanks as he passed them but was left alone to consider his inheritance and the fruit of his labor that had built upon that inheritance. "Work hard, and you'll get ahead, son," he could hear his father's voice. He lived by that axiom and found pleasure in handling the finances associated with a booming trade business. He had traveled and seen many wonders in the world, but returning to his home and his heritage always left him puzzled. He had attained all that anyone had ever dreamed of and had done so with a blameless life of honesty and integrity. He was respected by his community and at such a young age. Yet he always felt driven to something more.

He had decided. He would go to one final extreme to try to find something more. Although he had been away, he was not unaware of the stir around a man named Jesus, a common carpenter from Nazareth. Some claimed he was a great prophet, others the Messiah himself, but all agreed he spoke and taught like no man ever before.

The young man pushed away his plate and hurried to find this carpenter-turned-Rabbi. He strode through the streets and found him near the edge of town. The sight of him made him stop. An ordinary, weathered man, the Rabbi wore no rabbinic robe with tassels and long sleeves as the Pharisees did. People gathered about him and nudged their children toward him or held them up to receive a blessing. Jesus gathered one child into his arms and smiled on him, blessing the boy. The lad laid his head on Jesus' shoulder as if he wanted to rest there a long time. And the rich young man watched, wondering why he wished to be that child, to receive that blessing, to rest from this searching. Afraid he would miss his chance, he ran the rest of the way to Jesus and fell on his knees before him.

"Good teacher, what must I do to inherit eternal life?"

Jesus stopped and touched the young man's head, as he had done to the child. It made him feel like a little boy again.

"Only God is good, and you know his commandments."

"Yes, Teacher. I've kept them all since I was little." At this, the young man looked up to Jesus with a look that seemed to say, "Please, tell me there's more to it than that. The laws leave me empty." As Jesus looked into the man's eyes, the man was flooded with the love of God, and he knew he had found what he was longing for.

"One thing you lack," Jesus said. The man knew what it was. He wanted what Jesus had. He wanted this love that drew him near. He needed this sense of belonging and acceptance.

"What, Teacher?"

"Go sell everything you have. Give it to the poor, and you will have even greater treasures in heaven. Then come and follow me."

The man's heart sank. Surely he wasn't serious. After all, he had obeyed God's commands without fault while he maintained his business and household. Why must he give it up now? He rose from his knees, dusted off his robe and looked away from Jesus, not wanting to be reminded of what he was giving up. He turned, head down in sorrow, and slowly walked away empty.

HIDDEN JOY

Consider the meditation on the story of the rich young ruler and record your thoughts in your journal:

- Describe the test or temptation the rich young man faced. What was he really looking for? What was Jesus really asking the rich young man when he suggested that he sell his riches and give the money to the poor?

- Imagine that the young man had taken Jesus' suggestion. What would the victory have looked like? How did the young man experience defeat? How do you think this encounter affected the rest of his life?

- In what part of this man's pilgrimage do you see yourself: Wondering if there is something more? On your way toward Jesus? On your knees in dialogue with Jesus? Walking away from Jesus? Choosing instead to follow him? Once you have identified where you are, write out a prayer to God about your experience with him thus far. Do you still thirst for him in some way? Where is he calling you to go?

- Slowly read John 19 and 20. How do the cross and the empty tomb speak to you of defeat and victory? Which words or phrases stir your heart? What might God be revealing to you personally through these words? Now read Colossians 2:13-15. This is your triumph. Praise God for his grace at work in you.

8

THE SACRED . . .

in the Desert of Routines

We don't have to go far to find the treasure we are seeking. There is beauty and goodness right where we are. And only when we can see the beauty and goodness that are close by can we recognize beauty and goodness on our travels far and wide. There are trees and flowers to enjoy, paintings and sculptures to admire. Most of all there are people who smile, play, and show kindness and gentleness. They are all around us, to be recognized as free gifts to receive in gratitude.

HENRI NOUWEN, *BREAD FOR THE JOURNEY*

QUIET YOUR HEART

Read Psalm 100. Let the joy of the Lord inhabit your heart, soul and mind. Take time to sing or listen to music today as you worship with joyful songs.

ENTER HIS PRESENCE

Read Psalm 104, and meditate on God's delight in his creation. Consider how everything he creates he engages for his holy purposes. As you consider God's thoughtful plan for creation, sing a song of praise to him.

Spiritual deserts do not always arrive on the doorstep of catastrophe. Often the mundane routines and trivial problems taunt me like a desert dust devil, that little whirlwind of dirt and debris that stirs up my days with minor irritations and tosses specks of grit in my eyes—getting stuck behind a slow driver when I am in a hurry, arriving two minutes after the bank closes, forgetting to put the washed clothes in the drier, losing the car keys. None of these typical frustrations puts me into crisis mode, but unless I discipline my heart to stay focused on God, the tiny troubles can mushroom into thunderheads of resentment.

On other days, life marches along, never missing a stride in the daily routine. No surprises, no challenges, no change, and suddenly I am drifting into a tasteless mixture of boredom and complacency. In either scenario—the tiny troubles or the routine ruts—I miss the holy ground and sacred steps I trod on pilgrimage with God.

My weekly trip to a local coffeehouse has become an intentional act of sacramental living in the flow of my ordinary days. It is during these rest stops where I have often met God. My favorite hangout is the Coffee Rush. The young people who work there seem to care about the clientele, each other and their jobs. They like the title *barista* and have held that position for longer than I think I would have stuck with it. They love to take their breaks on the patio near the lakefront where they chat and compare their latest tattoos and dreams of the future. They laugh a lot, appreciate music and seem relaxed with who they are. And though they may not personally know God, they possess the fundamental attitudes of sacramental living—an awareness of the value and beauty of life.

By watching them, I am reminded to seek God in the pure reality of living day in and day out—to look for the sacred while reading the Sunday newspaper or dealing with the Monday-morning blues. Living with a sense of the sacred is the first step in the continuous journey of prayer, that ongoing spirit-to-Spirit dialogue that occurs even as we work, play, eat, sleep or stop at the local coffeehouse.

GOD IN THE ORDINARY

Jesus was the master of sacramental living, taking ordinary moments or objects and seeing God's message unfold in them. He knew God when he picked up a coin, when he observed sheep and vineyards or a city set on a hill, when he planted mustard seeds and interacted with rebellious children. He sensed God's leading while attending weddings and funerals, watching a fig tree or smelling the fragrance of perfume. He considered the lessons of whitewashed tombs, good neighbors, a fallen sparrow, lilies of the field, a towel and basin, water in a well, the bread and the wine, and the bitter drink he'd rather not taste.

By seeing God in the ordinary, he walked with God in the splendor of his glory. He brought God down to earth, literally and figuratively, opening the way for you and me to coexist with God. We too can develop this extraordinary view of life that Christ possessed by knowing and experiencing God around us, God in us and we in God. I used to think of these truths as a progression in spiritual maturity, but the more I consider it, the more I see it as a threefold revelation of God in Father, Son and Holy Spirit, speaking the unceasing reality of "God with us." Let me share what I mean through three sacred moments from my own ordinary days.

God around me. I had driven the road to work a hundred times before, a quiet highway, off the beaten path of freeway traffic, that cuts through the Arizona desert toward a small farming community. But on this spring morning, following a heavy rain the night before, the sun met the cool desert ground and fog began to form. Fog in the desert. I have lived in Arizona for over thirty years and know it is a rare sight. So I paid careful attention to details and listened intently for God's voice. The desert in radiant spring bloom, blanketed in fog—I felt like I was traveling through a watercolor masterpiece.

As the sun tried to filter though the dense veil, its reflection formed a rainbow effect to the right rear of my car. Every time I glanced to the right, that little rainbow pursued me. I wondered if traffic etiquette or ordinance required that I yield for rainbows. On I drove, delighting in the unusual beauty, until l found my dirt-road turnoff. Only today it was a mud road, and my car fishtailed this way and that, spitting mud droplets from the tires onto the windshield. My fingers gripped the steering wheel tighter as I prayed for God to keep me out of the nearby irrigation ditches.

Finally at my destination, I marveled that in less than an hour

I had traveled through nearly every type of road condition possible, a symbol of my path toward God. Some days I am traveling a fast pace on a smooth, sunny freeway. Other days slow me down as I recapture the beauty of life. And then there are those treacherous times when I wonder if I will make it through unharmed. But when I look back over the journey, holding fast to God, I see he was with me all the way, reaching out to me in all the wonder of his creation. "For since the creation of the world God's invisible qualities—his eternal power and divine nature—have been clearly seen, being understood from what has been made, so that men are without excuse" (Romans 1:20).

God in me. When I sense God in me, I have the power to change my outlook on ordinarily frustrating circumstances—like when I am dealing with people who are habitually late. One day I found sacred ground as I waited in a bagel shop at 7:00 a.m. to meet a friend who isn't a morning person. I knew from the get-go that she probably wouldn't show, but I arrived as an act of faith to her and to God. It is during these early mornings that I covenant with God and he covenants with me to meet and greet the day.

I watch people shuffle through the door and smile as they enter this morning gathering place. Two little redheaded boys arrive in their jammies with grandma. "This is an adventure," their faces say. One clutches a bottle and blankie, ready to tackle anything that may come his way. Then a middle-aged businessman enters. He nods at me, acknowledging our mutual existence in space and time. He speaks a hushed greeting of "Morning." I respond in kind, marveling in the one-word, here-and-now miracle that we awake and breathe, rise with the sun and make our own trek through another twenty-four

hours. The cashier—definitely a morning person—is hearty in
his morning greetings and waves and calls out, "How ya' doin'?"
when the door swings open again.

In the waiting, I sense God in me and thank him for the brilliance of morning and rich, black drink and doughy bagels, for
the nods and smiles and hearty hellos, for the friends who
aren't morning people and don't show, and for faith that knows
that these good and perfect gifts come down from the Father
of the heavenly lights—the Father of morning sunshine and
earthly morning greetings and who changes my dark irritation
into a dawning of delight.

Me in God. When I actually get to a point in my ordinary day
where I realize that the world does not revolve around me,
then I can rest in the truth that God has enfolded me in his
arms and invited me into his purposes. At first glance, this
seems a more difficult reality to grasp, but in fact, it may be
more difficult to explain because it is the most simple. As
Christ-followers, we are always and continuously *in* God. The
challenge is to appreciate it in new and creative ways each day.

If I am created by God and for God, then life is pointless
without God. And if I am created to glorify God in every aspect of my daily life, then I can choose to live with a singleness
of purpose: to live for and in the glory of God. Author Victoria
Brooks says it well:

> What is the chief end of man? To glorify God and enjoy Him
> forever! With great rejoicing these words have become the
> theme of my existence. The woven word of God has wrapped
> me fully round and now I wear these simple sentences every-
> where. I never take them off. I sleep in the comfort of their
> closeness and walk with them through each new day. I never tire

of their pattern. I attend christenings and funerals alike in this single garment; and in this I will be buried, for it is what I want to be wearing when I meet Him face-to-face. I am sealed for all time in this apparel of praise, cloaked in the sure knowledge that I do not exist for me at all. I have been created for God.[1]

These snapshots of the sacred, the holy moments we long for each day, reflect a desire to know God, to sense his presence and to follow his leading. Perhaps it was an awareness of this simple beauty of a life hidden in God that led the psalmist to write and pray:

> My heart is not proud, O LORD,
>   my eyes are not haughty;
> I do not concern myself with great matters
>   or things too wonderful for me.
> But I have stilled and quieted my soul;
>   like a weaned child with its mother,
>   like a weaned child is my soul within me. (Psalm 131:1-2)

REST STOP

Reflect on the past twenty-four to forty-eight hours. Make a list of the routine events of those hours. Consider any activity that could be viewed as a symbol of God's character. Or perhaps it was a time that you simply became aware of the uniqueness or beauty in something or someone.

RIVERS OF DELIGHT

Sacramental living requires a waking faith, a watch-and-pray faith, a pay-attention faith. It takes training to see God in the ordinary, and it requires a desire to contemplate his presence, to seek and see the holy in the art of living.

Perhaps more than any other aspect of life, a meal holds great symbols of the sacred even today. Many stories of Christ take place over a meal—feeding the 5,000 on a hillside, dinner with Simon the leper, breaking bread with two followers in Emmaus, breakfast on the beach. And how appropriate a setting for the one who called himself the Bread of Life. But the meal most sacred to believers today is Christ's "Last Supper"— reenacted in the giving and receiving in the sacrament of Communion, or the Eucharist.

The story that plays out in the upper room unfolds layer upon layer of sacramental living. The Passover, rich with meaning and symbols of Hebrew history and faith, overlays the new covenant with symbols of wine and bread—taken, blessed, broken and shared. All three gospels that outline the details of the Last Supper list Christ's actions at the table in this order. And it was this fourfold sacred act that Henri Nouwen, a great spiritual guide to this generation, observed as symbolic truth for our lives today as we become God's beloved.

Taken. "Jesus took the bread." He chose it as a symbol, just as we too have been chosen by God. One ordinary encounter in my own life reminded me of my "chosenness" as I stood next to a woman in a local department store. Surveying the merchandise, I reached past her to examine an item on the shelf then turned to leave. But as I did, the woman surprisingly called to me, "Marsha?"

The instant she said my name, even before I turned to look, I knew her as a woman I had worked with many years earlier. "Laura!" I cried in disbelief. We hugged and laughed for not recognizing each other, reminisced over happy days in the workplace and caught up on family developments. Later I pondered that moment when we finally saw one another. Something about her voice had triggered a recognition my other senses had missed. It had cut through my preoccupied and distracted state of mind. Only by the sound of her voice calling my name was I reunited with my old friend.

It happened to Mary Magdalene too. There by the empty tomb, she wept. She saw Jesus but was too distracted by her sorrow to recognize him standing so near. When he called her name, "Mary," her spirit awoke, and she knew and worshiped her risen Lord. But it all hinged on Jesus speaking her name. God tells his chosen people:

> I summon you by name
>   and bestow on you a title of honor. (Isaiah 45:4)

His desire to take us as his chosen ones is reflected in the names he bestows on us in Scripture—names of endearment and encouragement that bring his honor into our lives. With confidence I can claim that I am the apple of his eye (Psalm 17:8), the sheep of his pasture (Psalm 100:3), his beautiful one (Song of Songs 2:10), his bride (Song of Songs 4:8), the garden of his delight (Isaiah 5:7), the ransomed of the Lord (Isaiah 35:10), an iron pillar (Jeremiah 1:18), his friend (John 15:13-14), a new creation (2 Corinthians 5:17), Christ's ambassador (2 Corinthians 5:20), the temple of the living God (2 Corinthians 6:16), an heir (Galatians 4:7), his workmanship (Ephesians 2:10), and the list goes on and on. In a world that wants to lump us together into a one-size-fits-all marketplace and with a government that prefers to call us by number, God took us as his own, chose us before we even knew how to love him, called us each by name, and we became his beloved.

The great spiritual battle begins—never to end—with the re-
claiming of our chosenness. Long before any human being saw
us, we were seen by God's loving eyes. Long before any one
heard us cry or laugh, we were heard by our God who is all ears
for us. Long before any person spoke to us in this world, we
were spoken to by the voice of eternal love. Our preciousness,
uniqueness and individuality were not given to us by those who
meet us in clock-time . . . but by the one who has chosen us with
an everlasting love, a love that existed from all eternity and that
will last through all eternity.[2]

Blessed. What does it mean to be blessed? Blessing, contrary
to popular thought, does not mean life is going well in every
way. When someone receives a big promotion, a new car or financial windfall, we often hear, "God's really blessed me." And
I always wonder where that leaves me as I attempt to make my
tiny income stretch over my budget without ripping.

The true meaning of being blessed comes from the Latin
that means "to speak well"; it is the word we use for "benedic-
tion." It is what Jesus did at the Last Supper when he prayed
over his disciples and over his future disciples, you and me. He
spoke good words to the Father on our behalf, and we need
such blessings, not only from him but also from one another, in
order to recognize the holiness of God in our own lives.

For me, one of the most meaningful moments in my local
church comes when we share the Lord's Table. Occasionally,
rather than passing the bread and juice on silver trays, our pastor invites us up to the table to receive the sacraments. We
come with one or two others to take the symbols of the blood
and broken body of Christ. Then our pastor puts his arms
around us and prays for us as individuals. From this encounter
I always leave with a sense of healing and completeness, loved

by the Father through the Son and through his bride, the church. This type of blessing and communion service always takes longer to reenact, but all eagerly wait for the body, the blood and the blessing of love in order to become the beloved.

Broken. When we receive Christ's broken body, we also stop to look at our own broken lives. This is the part we want to skip over, but until our broken lives are placed in the Savior's hands, we simply lie in meaningless pieces, disconnected and disjointed. "Our brokenness open[s] us to a deeper way of sharing our lives and offering each other hope. Just as bread needs to be broken in order to be given, so, too, do our lives."[3] David realized this in his psalm of confession over his adulterous and murderous life (Psalm 51). God doesn't want a flashy show of sacrifice or offering; he desires our broken spirits and contrite hearts. But it is difficult to break open hearts that seem hard as rock.

I am reminded of Moses in the wilderness and the Hebrews grumbling against him and God for lack of water. They were thirsty, but their hearts were hard. So God instructed Moses to strike the rock with his staff. And when he did, water gushed out. We don't know if the rock was broken into pieces, cracked open or miraculously turned into water, but it was changed and refreshment flowed out.

As I meditated on this thought one day, I felt God calling me to bring him all the rocks I could find in my own life, those hard parts of my heart that needed his touch: rocks of prejudice, bad moods, cynicism, laziness and rebellion against caring for myself. And with each rock I brought, I confessed my sin and asked God to strike it and bring forth water of refreshment. And the more rocks I brought, the more the rocks were broken apart and the more fountains of love and mercy poured out, soaking my soul, cleansing my heart and healing my wounds. Brokenness leads us to repentance, and repentance to refreshment. "Repent, then, and turn to God, so that your sins may be wiped out, that times of refreshing may come from the Lord" (Acts 3:19).

Shared. We are ready to share with others only when our rocky hearts have been turned to water. Then, like Paul, we can say, "I am already being poured out like a drink offering" (2 Timothy 4:6). And from God's mercy poured out on me, I can in turn offer it to others.

A friend came to my home with something on her mind. She was fidgeting nervously and seemed almost frightened. "I have to tell you something. I've never told anyone else . . . it may change what you think of me . . . it may change our friendship, but I have to share it because I believe God wants me to." For the next thirty minutes I listened to my friend tell me about the abortion of her first child when she was a college student. She cried as she spoke, and her hands were shaking. She poured herself out of a bottled-up world of poisoned thoughts and memories that she had held inside for too long, afraid of the truth, afraid of being rejected.

When she finished, I didn't know for sure what to say. I'm no counselor, but as is true for all believers, I hold the gift of grace and have been entrusted with the ministry of reconciliation. I remembered Jesus speaking words to his fearful disciples after the resurrection. He said, "'Peace be with you!' . . . and with that he breathed on them and said, 'Receive the Holy Spirit. If you forgive anyone his sins, they are forgiven'" (John 20:21-23). So I held my friend close and told her how loved she is by God. In Jesus' name, I offered forgiveness. And as we shared together, she her hurt, me God's mercy, I knew God's pleasure rested on us both simply for the sharing.

REST STOP

Which of these four sacramental movements have you experienced in your own life? Which do you long for? Where do you see yourself right now?

Such sacred moments come to us from all directions—around us, in us and through us. God's omniscient Spirit inhabits broken hearts and holy hands that are lifted to him in prayer and praise. Then each day of ordinary life becomes the sanctuary where we enter the Holy of Holies and experience the glory that flows from the mercy seat. This cycle of being taken, blessed, broken and shared repeats itself sometimes on a daily basis, sometimes through broader seasons of life, but each step is a sacred reality of our pilgrimage with God who transforms the mundane routines and trivial problems into holy ground.

A DESERT JOURNEY

Read Matthew 17:1-13, and picture this scene in your mind:

> *It was a long, steep climb. Their legs and arms ached from pushing their muscles to keep pace with the Master. They were too breathless to complain, but finally they came to a level clearing. A lone olive tree grew from the rock and provided shade and a place to lean their backs and close their eyes. But as Peter, James and John rested, a breeze and a brilliance penetrated their fatigued souls. Suddenly their tired bodies tensed with fear. Their Lord appeared radiant, so brilliant, in fact, that they shaded their eyes, unable to look fully upon his face. He was not alone. Standing near him were two*

other men enveloped by the radiance of Jesus. The three talked together. Their conversation revealed them to be Moses and Elijah.

James and John sat dumbfounded, unable to find words in the midst of this heavenly meeting. But Peter, always ready for action, presented his plan to Jesus. Like a child wanting to put the ocean in a bottle to save forever, he said, "Lord, this is too good to be true. Let me put up three tent shelters for you, Moses and Elijah."

But God himself intervened. The God who cannot be contained in a tent descended on them all and surrounded them in a brilliant, white cloud. His voice rumbled from within, "This is my Son, whom I love; with him I am well pleased. Listen to him." The three, even Peter, fell face down, eyes shut tight, hands over their heads, and trembled at the omnipotent majesty of their God.

As quickly as their world had changed, it returned to earthly reality. A hand touched each of them, and tender words soothed their troubled hearts. "Get up. Don't be afraid." It was Jesus, alone, looking like the ordinary man from Nazareth they knew and loved. Amazement, questions, delight and strength filled them all. Too much to comprehend just now but enough mystery to think on for years to come—how holiness met humanity and transfigured ordinary life into heaven's majestic glory.

HIDDEN JOY

- Spend a few minutes with your eyes closed, meditating on what this moment must have been like for the three disciples. What do your senses see, hear, smell, touch or taste as you witness this heavenly scene? Write down these images in your journal.

- Peter referred to this incident in his letter to the early church. Read his recollection of the transfiguration in 2 Peter 1:16-18. How do you think this changed his ordinary life into a sacred reality?

- Read 1 John 1:1-4. John uses his own experiences and senses to testify to the good news of Christ. What reasons does he give for finding the sacred in the ordinary? How have you, or how can you, do this with the people you interact with on a daily basis?

- Make a one-column list of six ordinary events you experience every day. In an adjoining column, write down any thoughts about how this routine task can open your eyes to God. (For example, "Every red light I encounter on my way to work will remind me to stop and offer a prayer of thanksgiving." Or, "When I open the mail I will consider what message God would write to me at that moment if the envelope contained a card from him.")

9

RESURRECTION . . .

in the Desert of Death

*The early morning belongs to the Church of the risen Christ.
At the break of light it remembers the morning on which
death and sin lay prostrate in defeat and new life and salvation
were given to mankind.*

DEITRICH BONHOEFFER, *LIFE TOGETHER*

QUIET YOUR HEART

Forget the former things;
   do not dwell on the past.
See, I am doing a new thing!
   Now it springs up; do you not perceive it?
I am making a way in the desert
   and streams in the wasteland. (Isaiah 43:18-19)

ENTER HIS PRESENCE

Read Song of Songs 2:10-13 as if it were spoken by the lover of your soul, Jesus
Christ. Consider how he calls you to arise and come into a place of fruitfulness.
Enjoy the delight he has in being joined with his beloved in celebration of this
new season of plenty.

I SPENT A LONG PERIOD OF TIME MOURNING MY BROKEN marriage, the loss of love, companionship, family unity and intimacy. With time I also felt God's tender call to "come forth" as he once called Lazarus back from death into new life. But I did not know if I was ready. Never would I move ahead without God's release to do so. So that fall I took some time alone in the mountains of northern New Mexico to pray and be still before God as I sought his face.

"I need a sign, Lord." Rarely did I ask for one, but on this I had to be certain. I listened and watched for his prompting all weekend but didn't perceive any direct leading. I loaded up my car and headed toward the highway but wanted to make one last stop on my way out of the retreat center. I pulled over to the side of the road and walked up a path into the tranquility of a beautiful prayer garden. Two rows of towering white aspens swayed as a strong breeze rustled through the branches. Sunshine-yellow leaves began to fall, riding the wind, and rained down on me in bunches. I looked up into that brilliant, leafy blizzard and laughed and cried all at once. I held out my hands, twirled in the leaf drifts at my feet and danced with the wind. He left no doubt. His Spirit moved me, like a breeze tugging on leaves, to let go of the past and fall into his loving arms. But I wondered how.

THE FIRST STEP

As inviting as new life sounds and as enticing as a fresh start looks, it only happens when we are willing to step into the darkness of death. The old must depart for the new to arrive, and the past must fade for the future to shine. Just before the dawn, we step into the desert's dark night once more and wait for Jesus to stand in our midst and call us to "come forth" into new life with him.

It is natural to resist change, even when it's an invitation to a fresh start. After the disciples peered into the empty tomb, they still found it difficult to move forward in faith. Instead we see that rough bunch hiding, shrouded by fear, doubts and failure. We too may have the same reactions as we begin to embrace new life with Christ.

Disturbed by doubts. Like Thomas, some Christians rest comfortably in their doubts about God's faithfulness, about his Spirit at work in the church, about the reality of a resurrected Savior. Every congregation has a Thomas who doesn't want to be proved the fool, who has an I-told-you-so response tucked in his pocket, always ready to use. It is the "show-me-the-money" individual who never takes a step of faith without first knowing how it will all turn out in the end. They attribute every provision, every healing and every answered prayer to the work of humans, or if it can't be proven, then the "coincidence factor" always plays well. As much as they complain about the spiritual desert, they have grown comfortable there and even enjoy the familiarity of a barren and fruitless faith.

That is how the Israelites reacted when they reached their Promised Land. "It's too scary . . . too risky. Let's turn back and stay in our wilderness."

Disconnected from the body. Maybe, like Mary Magdalene crying alone at the empty tomb, we have disconnected ourselves from the body of believers. We would rather live a solo faith than sing in the choir of hypocrites. That better-than-the-crowd attitude can quickly turn to the attention-getting ruse of self-pity and playing the victim. And although we are all fed by daily, personal time with God, many Christians get stuck there and merely tolerate the church at large and the fellowship of believers. While Jesus recognized Mary's deep love for him, he redirected that devotion back to the gathering of believers to be poured out to the other disciples, where the essence of Christ's spirit would now dwell.

Distracted by others. Perhaps, like Peter, we are distracted by someone else's spiritual life. Even in the midst of a quiet walk by the lake with Jesus, Peter was looking back, questioning Jesus about *John's* future. We can get hung up in one of two ways by this distraction: Some fret that others are more spiritual, more attuned to God, more devout than they, so they waste their time comparing spiritual gifts rather than using them to strengthen the body. Others look at their fellow Christians from a pedestal of "spiritual maturity," wishing the weaker brothers and sisters were as committed as they. Either way, we are looking in the wrong direction. Peering over my shoulder at the person in the pew behind me means I have taken my eyes off of Jesus.

God always calls us to move forward in our walk with him, to be willing to risk, to become vulnerable, to trust, to let go and to move forward. It is what Paul did when he said, "Forgetting what is behind and straining toward what is ahead, I press on toward the goal to win the prize for which God has called me heavenward in Christ Jesus" (Philippians 3:13-14). God only calls us to look back so we can remember his goodness and glory as a motivator to move forward in faith once more. The movement of life for any Christ-follower is always onward. This is an indicator of a thriving spiritual life. Moving forward is the byproduct of hope and the fruit of faith. But what is it we move out of? Out of despair, out of loneliness, out of dissatisfaction and out of confusion. He is a God who always leads us out.

REST STOP

Identify the way you most frequently resist new life in Christ. What steps can you take to remove this obstacle and bring about a change in your attitude and actions? Write a prayer of confession about your resistance and rebellion to new growth.

RIVERS OF DELIGHT

It is interesting and of no coincidence that the encounters Jesus had after the resurrection always occurred with two or more believers. In the case of Mary alone at the tomb, he instructed her to return to the group as well. Here is the seed of unity in the church and a key to living life anew. We simply cannot make it alone.

There are those unique exceptions when Christians have been cut off in isolation from the church; but undoubtedly their faith stayed strong only as far as their knowledge that the church at large was praying with them, singing psalms, hymns and spiritual songs, and hoping in a future where together they would reign with God. Dietrich Bonhoeffer, a German theologian and pastor, found himself in such a position after participating in a conspiracy to assassinate Adolf Hitler. Before his execution, he wrote from his prison cell in 1945, "Blessed is he who is alone in the strength of the fellowship and blessed is he who keeps the fellowship in the strength of aloneness."[1]

We cannot fully see Christ without joining ourselves to the body of Christ. "But the church is my problem," you may say. That is like saying church would be great if it weren't for the people. Bonhoeffer's words again speak to this: "Our relationship to God is a new life in existence for others, through participation in the being of Jesus. . . . The church is the church only when it exists for others."[2] In fact, it is in the lives of ordinary, sinful, grace-needy people where Christ is at work, leading us out of the tombs of darkness and into the light of new life together.

He leads us from doubt to devotion. Countless fingers have long pointed to Thomas as the example of what *not* to do in our faith. But in the midst of the doubts, Jesus never condemned Thomas but encouraged him with strong, simple words, "Stop doubting and believe." Of course it was easy for the others to believe because they had already seen Christ alive and well.

What Thomas teaches me is that I need to thirst for my own experience with Christ. He didn't settle for secondhand faith. He longed to know the resurrected Lord for himself. Isn't this what we all long for, an experience that makes us cry out, "My Lord and my God"? But Thomas was led from doubt to devotion because others first pointed the way. He never would have longed to see Jesus for himself if he hadn't seen it in others.

God gives us one another to stir our spirits, to make us thirst and to lead us to the living waters. Always there is someone who has experienced a new depth of Christ's presence beyond our current experience with Christ. Always there are deeper waters to tread in his grace. Thus when we recognize Christ in our midst, we want to worship him together. And by our acts of corporate worship and sharing our faith, we reveal Christ to others who then begin to thirst anew for his touch.

He leads us from singularity to unity. Back home on the shores of the Sea of Galilee, at least seven of the apostles sat wondering what to do next. So, in a statement of singularity, Peter announced his own intentions, "I'm going out to fish" (John 21:3). The six others agreed to go along for the ride. They spent the night on the water and, as so often seemed the case, had no luck fishing. I can almost hear them complaining, tired, irritable, and beginning to blame each other for their failure.

But then a wonderful word is thrown into their midst like a net cast into the sea. Coming from the shore, they hear the call, "Friends." And all look up and out in one direction. "Friends, haven't you caught any fish?" It almost sounds like a good-natured rub—a reminder of how a carpenter had once taught some fishermen how to fish, a mirrored reflection of the past, but more than déjà vu.

As I meditate on this passage, I see two miracles occur beyond the tremendous catch of fish. First, this scene not only points out the strength of each man but also reveals how each individual, with special qualities and abilities, fits together in a puzzle of unity when they all face toward Jesus. They move from singularity, and perhaps self-centeredness, to unity and Christ-centeredness. "For Jesus Christ alone is our unity. 'He is our peace.' Through him alone do we have access to one another, joy in one another, and fellowship with one another."[3]

It was John who first recognized Christ and pointed the others toward him. Peter's reckless faith inspires us to dive in with total commitment. Some were called to row the boat together. Others hung onto the net full of fish and brought it to shore. Each was given a purpose as a result of knowing Christ and obeying his call to come, united as one, with what they had to give as individuals.

The second, and perhaps greatest, miracle comes with Jesus' first word to them: "Friends." He calls us collectively into intimate friendship with him. Together we share the meal on the beach and bring the fruit of our labor to him. Jesus already had hot coals, fish and bread of his own to offer. Still he invites us to bring what we have as well. This is the partnership of friends working together for one purpose: to come to the fire of burning coals where we experience the passion of companionship with Jesus, and there we are changed as he leads us out of our own agenda and into his.

He leads us from failure to fresh starts. In an intimate conversation on a walk along the beach, Jesus never brings up Peter's threefold failure of denial prior to the crucifixion. Instead, he offers Peter three opportunities to embrace him as never before with the incessant question that pierces our hearts still today, "Do you love me?" He knew Peter's propensity toward action and work but insisted that it always be anchored in his love for him. Only Christ's love can conquer our failure:

> for love is as strong as death,
>   its jealousy unyielding as the grave.
> It burns like blazing fire,
>   like a mighty flame. (Song of Songs 8:6)

In the end, Peter walked with Jesus once again in intimate friendship, leaving behind his failure.

"You must follow me," Jesus said. For Peter, there had to be a sense of coming full circle in this pilgrimage with Christ. Jesus' words sounded like that first call so long ago to follow him, but this time something was different. The old call was to come to Jesus and follow along behind him, to learn of him. This call to follow holds a new meaning, like two travelers in union on a road, fellow pilgrims walking together and working together in a lasting, loving bond of friendship. This isn't the old way of following hard on Jesus' heels. It is a shoulder-to-shoulder striding on a new pathway of life. I can almost see the old passing away and the new life emerging in Peter.

A seed entombed in the dark earth dies, leaving behind its old form and awakening a new form that pushes toward the light. So too are our lives firmly planted in Christ. We sow tears and reap songs of joy (Psalm 126:5); we sow doubt and reap acts of devotion (John 20:28); we sow pain and reap fields of grace (2 Corinthians 12:7-9). And from our new life, we grow and produce the fruit of joy, devotion and grace and begin the cycle of praise all over again.

REST STOP

How do you relate to these areas of new life where Christ leads us? Has he lead you from one point that seemed spiritually fulfilling into a new place that reveals greater depths of his love? Can you discern other aspects of your life that need resurrecting? Write a prayer about this need, and seek God's counsel to experience new life.

I too had a sense of coming full circle. Months earlier I had gradually descended from the mountaintop into my desert dwelling. Now with the promise of new life, I realized I was back in the fresh, crisp air of the mountains again. I scooped up a handful of fallen leaves, buttery gold with crimson flecks, and considered taking them home as a reminder of this precious moment and direction from God. But even that gesture felt like holding onto the past, so I let them drift back to the ground again. I inhaled that damp-leaf autumn scent once more and turned to head home. For the first time in a long time, an excitement about my life pushed its way through my conscious thoughts, and I prayed, "Lord, I'm ready to come forth."

A DESERT JOURNEY

Read Luke 24:13-35, and picture this scene in your mind:

Heads down, hearts low, two men walked home, feeling the weight of disappointment and disillusionment. Maybe talking about the whole ordeal would ease the burden. So they began to recount the days in Jerusalem leading up to the cruel death of their beloved teacher and friend. With each step on the dusty road, they stirred up memories, trying to determine where they had gone wrong. The certainty of Jesus being the Chosen One, the very Son of God, their Messiah, had burned into their hearts and minds.

But now they felt betrayed and alone. "If he is the Christ, then why did he die a criminal's death?"

"How could he have died at all?" Their questions were too heavy to wrestle into order, so silence now hung between them. On they walked, until another traveler stepped up unexpectedly to their side and journeyed with them toward their home in Emmaus. This stranger intrigued them as he asked, "What are you discussing?" So again they retold the events of their last days in Jerusalem. The stranger listened but then began to share from his own heart, interpreting the Scriptures as he spoke. He took their discus-

sion to a new depth of consideration. He challenged them in their under-standing of the prophetic writings.

The long road home passed too quickly. Evening fell as they arrived in Em-maus. "Please, stay with us," they urged the stranger, because they hungered to continue this conversation. And so he stayed. They prepared a simple meal and sat down to eat. The stranger, as though he were the host and they his guests, took the bread, broke it and passed it to his two companions. As they received it and began to eat, their eyes were opened and their hearts quickened when they recognized their Savior. And in that instant he was gone, leaving the two alone, breathless and stammering in their excitement. At the same time, they were humbled that their living Lord had chosen to visit them.

It couldn't have been a dream, for they both recalled the same reality. And they recognized the passion in their heart for Jesus, rekindled to burn brighter than ever before. It sent them out again, even into the darkness of night, to testify of new life in them both and good news for the world.

HIDDEN JOY

- What activities, observations or circumstances have made your "heart burn within you," knowing you were in Christ's pres-ence? (Luke 24:32).

- Reread the Scripture passage of this story (Luke 24:13-35). De-scribe the attitude and physical demeanor of the two at the be-ginning of the story compared to the end. What can you discern about their change? In what ways did Christ lead them out or call them to come forth?

- Read Psalm 149 aloud to the Lord as your song of new life. Choose a word or phrase from this psalm and rewrite your own song or prayer based on it. Let God turn your wailing into dancing so that your heart "may sing . . . and not be silent" (Psalm 30:12).

EPILOGUE

You don't have to travel far into the desert before you will encounter a pile of bones—cattle, javelina, coyote or jackrabbit—bleached white by the sun. Dry bones like Ezekiel saw in his revelation from God. These images remind us that we entered the desert feeling scattered and disjointed, lifeless and useless, like a sun-bleached skeleton. But after God has spoken, we see how he reconnects body to spirit, how he breathes new life into rattling bones and how flesh and soul sing and dance as one.

But I'm not sure there is ever one moment or event that brings us from the desert back into the Promised Land. Usually it comes when we stop trying to leave and realize that God is in this place, that the dry heat lifts and the desert blooms again. Not that suddenly everything is rosy. We still have times when the sun blazes and the thorn scratches. But when we reassess our condition and our relationship with God, we can begin to dance in the desert as I imagine Jesus must have done when the devil left and the angels arrived to minister to him in the wilderness.

When I began my desert journey, I assumed that I would eventually leave with much wisdom and direction to share

with others. But the reality is that there are no answers to the
desert perplexities. Instead there is a soft echoing down canyon walls, a hushed resounding from God that reverberates
his assurance that he lives in the desert and in the waters, and
it all blurs together into one image of God. It is as Craig
Childs explains of his desert roots: "My mother was born be-
side a spring in the high desert. . . . The water from the spring
bathed and filled her body, tightening each of her cells. It
filled the hollow of her bones. Years later, as the water passed
from mother to child . . . I grew up thinking that water and
the desert were the same."[1]

I may even venture so far as to say that the soul thirst *is*
God—calling, drawing and leading deeper into the desert. It
is the same reality the psalmist spoke of when remembering
the Red Sea crossing: "He led them through the depths as
through a desert" (Psalm 106:9). I like to imagine myself in
that throng with the children of Israel, pushing my way to
the outer edge of the dry seabed, where I would run my fin-
gertips through the liquid wall as I passed by, feeling the miracle of my hand in the water as I scuffed my feet through the
desert floor. Whether it was the water they saw or the dry
ground where they walked, they knew it was caused by the
hand of God, the one who would someday reveal himself as
Living Water.

This is the God I have come to thirst for each day, and I realize that the more I partake of his life-giving love, the more I
desperately long for more. My thirst grows in direct proportion
to my ability to drink. And while I know God will never let me
die of thirst, I also know I will never be fully satisfied until I
meet him face to face and dwell with him and see "the river of

the water of life, as clear as crystal, flowing from the throne of God and of the Lamb down the middle of the great street of the city" (Revelation 22:1-2).

Filled with this hope, let's rejoice in the journey of today. Let's lift tambourines and voices and join in the desert dance. Let the children of God rejoice!

Appendix

Journaling the Journey

I keep a box full of mementos of my past—ticket stubs, birth announcements, newspaper clippings, funeral memorials, cards, letters, photographs and artwork made by my daughters' little hands. These fleeting remembrances testify to precious moments in my own life and remind me to "number my days aright" (Psalm 90:12).

Imagine if we could capture our memories with God and keep a glimmer of heaven in a box to peek at on occasion as a reminder of his grace. This is the very reason I have kept a spiritual journal for over fifteen years. My journals are filled with snapshots of God's presence intertwined with my life. Not every page reveals spiritual insights or miraculous moments. Some pages highlight trivialities, petty attitudes and to-do lists. But each page is directed toward God as an act of prayer. These bound words are a legacy of my faith pilgrimage. They speak, even to me, long after my memories fade. These signposts of my relationship with God reveal when I yielded, where I detoured, when I stopped and where I made directional choices.

Perhaps more than any other commitment, journaling has helped me move along in my development and conformity to Christ. It is the tool God uses to help me "break up the unplowed ground" of my soul (Hosea 10:12). While some would consider journaling a spiritual discipline, I view it as a vital tool in practicing those disciplines of prayer, meditation, solitude, worship and other avenues of meeting God. A journal fulfills two covenants that I made in my devotion to God long ago. These are the covenants of time and of place—physical symbols of my commitment to God.[1]

Knowing that he prepares a place and time for me too, I become his open vessel, willing to listen and receive from him. Some days he gives his insights and blessings. Often I am challenged, changed or checked in my spirit. Other days I simply come to worship, to acknowledge his might and majesty, his goodness and glory. But in the midst of a desert pilgrimage, I may simply wander in stillness and thirst for him more. The only "agenda" for my journal is to act as a receptacle for God's gifts of grace. I caution those who wish to begin journaling to let the journal remain God's tool of grace rather than your yoke of guilt. When we begin to worry "I haven't journaled today," then we miss the moments of grace that God has in store for us.

PREPARING TO JOURNAL THE JOURNEY

Often when I come to God in the quietness of my morning, hot coffee mug in hand, I find I cannot focus my thoughts on him. So even before I read, pray or study, I open my journal to accomplish one of three things:

Clear my mind. Some mornings, before my head even leaves the pillow, a load of worries and hassles wait for me to open my eyes. On such days I use my journal to clear my mind. This is not a magical method of liberation but simply a way to turn my heart toward God. This is the place where I unload the distractions. It usually doesn't take long because this isn't pretty writing, just dump-truck communication—pull in, dump the dirt and take off. But it is refreshing and soul lifting, and I am able to climb out from under the piled-up concerns and frustrations. Frequently I will come upon a new attitude or discovery about the distraction even as I write.

Stimulate my thoughts. On the opposite side of clearing my mind, I sometimes need my ideas and thoughts stirred up. In my journal I allow sights and sounds, observations and circumstances to blend together as the Master crafts his holiness into the reality of my days. It takes intentional reflection to find God's purpose and way at times. Just as water doesn't pump itself from the bottom of a well, so too reflection opens the valve to allow God's Spirit to flow through me and awake my mind to his presence.

Quiet my spirit. When life flies by and commitments leave little time to think straight, journaling puts my heart and mind into a slower gear, which allows me to see where I am traveling rather than letting it pass by in a blur. I can't write nearly as fast as I think or even speak. But when I journal, something happens inside that slowly unfolds my thoughts and reveals surprising pockets of hidden goodness in my day.

HOW TO JOURNAL THE JOURNEY

More than any other questions, people wonder, "What do I

write about, and how do I start?" Everyone has his or her own way to go about journaling. However, most people need a bit more direction when first starting out. There are as many different methods and ideas about journaling as there are people to write about them. You may want to journal to set goals, to unravel dreams or to work through a problem. Or you may want to keep a journal for each of your children. Some people keep separate prayer journals, study journals and travel journals. But I want to mention two types of journaling that have been the most helpful to me in my spiritual formation.

Reflective journaling. This is the type of ordinary writing that allows me to process what I see, hear, read and observe. It is a means of digesting and applying those things God uses to teach me his way. I gather the events of a day, spread them out onto the page and turn them all toward God. I explore my thoughts and feelings about this event or moment and search for God in the midst of it all. It is also the best exercise I know of to develop a lifestyle of unceasing prayer. What do I reflect? It may be a relational conflict, a paragraph from a book I am reading, a point from Sunday's sermon or a passing comment from a stranger. These are the things I write down, mull over and make my own.

Meditative journaling. The second method of journaling is also reflective, but looks specifically into Scripture. I love this contemplative discipline because I believe, as a friend once said, that my journal is a means of ministering to God. When my mind is filled with God's inspired words and I spend time deeply considering those words and images, then my heart is united to his. When I cast my gaze toward him, he delights in our connection and it pleases him.

Below is an exercise in meditative journaling that uses four simple steps adapted from Ronald Klug's book *How to Keep a Spiritual Journal.*[2]

Prepare the place. Gather Bible, journal and pen. If possible, find a quiet spot free from visual and audio distractions. Take a couple of deep breaths and release to God any worries, stress or anxiety clinging to your mind and heart. Now open your Bible and slowly begin to read the chosen Scripture passage. (We'll use Mark 7:31-37.) Reread it one more time, and let it open your heart to God. Madame Guyon, a seventeenth-century spiritual mystic, suggests, "Come before the Lord and begin to read. Stop reading when you feel the Lord drawing you inwardly to himself. Now, simply remain in stillness. Stay there for a while."[3]

Picture the scene. As you read the passage, what do you see? What do you hear, taste, smell and feel? Consider the scene from different points of view. Put yourself in the shoes of the deaf and mute man. See the scene and this man through Jesus' eyes. Step into the place of the people who brought this man to Jesus. Write down in your journal what you experience as you read these words.

Ponder the message. Which words, phrases, sentences and pictures speak to you in a meaningful way? What do you need to understand from these words for yourself, your family, your church or community? Is there a promise you can claim or a command to obey? Are there questions you need to ask God as you seek his wisdom? Write them down and wait on his leading.

Pray from the heart. Respond to God's voice, and pray a part of this Scripture for yourself. Rewrite any sentences or phrases in your own words as you speak, listen and wait on God.

Repeat this cycle every time you go to the Word. Practice using it as you read through the Gospels or meditate on the Psalms. Soon it will be a natural part of your devotion to God. Don't worry if at first journaling seems pointless or if you feel as if nothing is happening. Be content with the process as a means of honoring God and the covenant of time and place. Like farming, it takes time to prepare the soil and plant seeds, to water them and allow the light to shine on them until they're ready to grow and bear fruit. The days of contemplation and "useless" journaling are the means of preparing the ground of your heart and mind to receive God's word.

Finally, don't worry about a correct form or method as you journal. Simply know that God delights in your desire to meet him in this way, to open yourself up to his leading as you journal the journey with him and capture a glimmer of heaven here on earth.

NOTES

Introduction

[1] Craig Childs, *The Secret Knowledge of Water* (Seattle: Sasquatch, 2000), p. xvi.
[2] Jan Johnson, *When the Soul Listens* (Colorado Springs: NavPress, 1999), p. 179.

Chapter 1: Contentment . . . in the Desert of Desire

[1] Tricia McCary Rhodes, *Taking Up Your Cross: The Incredible Gain of the Crucified Life* (Minneapolis: Bethany House, 2000), p. 56.
[2] Richard Foster, introduction to Jean-Pierre de Caussade, *The Sacrament of the Present Moment* (San Francisco: HarperSanFrancisco, 1989), p. xx.

Chapter 2: Rest . . . in the Desert of Weariness

[1] Brother Lawrence, *The Practice of the Presence of God* (Springdale, Penn.: Whitaker House, 1982), pp. 20–21.
[2] Eugene Petersen, *Leap over a Wall* (New York: HarperCollins, 1998), p. 31.
[3] Renita Weems, *Listening to God* (New York: Simon & Schuster, 1999), p. 77.
[4] Howard Baker, *Soul Keeping: Ancient Paths of Spiritual Direction* (Colorado Springs: NavPress, 1998), pp. 125-26.

Chapter 3: Identity . . . in the Desert of Confusion

[1] Robert Benson, *Between the Dreaming and the Coming True* (New York: Jeremy P. Tarcher/Putnam, 1996).
[2] Teresa of Ávila, *The Interior Castle*, in *Majestic Is Your Name*, ed. David Hazard (Minneapolis: Bethany House, 1993), p. 36.
[3] Eugene Peterson, *Leap over a Wall* (San Francisco: HarperSanFrancisco, 1997), p. 187.
[4] Teresa of Ávila, *Interior Castle*, p. 36.

[5]David Wolpe, *Making Loss Matter* (New York: Riverhead, 1999), p. 113.
[6]Ken Gire, *The Reflective Life* (Colorado Springs: Chariot Victor, 1998), p. 86.
[7]Thomas à Kempis, *The Imitation of Christ* (London: Penguin, 1952), p. 98.

CHAPTER 4: LIGHT . . . IN THE DESERT OF DARKNESS

[1]*The Cloud of Unknowing*, in *The Spiritual Formation Bible* (Grand Rapids, Mich.: Zondervan, 1999), p. 565.
[2]John of the Cross, *Dark Night of the Soul* 1.14, in *You Set My Spirit Free*, ed. David Hazard (Minneapolis: Bethany House, 1995), pp. 83-84.
[3]Craig Barnes, *When God Interrupts* (Downers Grove, Ill.: InterVarsity Press, 1996), p. 17.
[4]Donald McCullough, *The Trivialization of God* (Colorado Springs: NavPress, 1995), pp. 13-14.
[5]Frederick Buechner, *The Hungering Dark* (New York: HarperCollins, 1985), p. 125.
[6]John of the Cross, *Dark Night*, pp. 83-84.

CHAPTER 5: RENEWAL . . . IN THE DESERT OF LOSS

[1]Henri Nouwen, *Reaching Out: The Three Movements of the Spiritual Life*, in *The Spiritual Formation Bible* (Grand Rapids, Mich.: Zondervan, 1999), p. 755.
[2]Sue Monk Kidd, *When the Heart Waits* (San Francisco: HarperCollins, 1992), p. 31.
[3]Andrew Murray, *The Believer's Secret of Waiting on God* (Minneapolis: Bethany House, 1986), pp. 132–33.

CHAPTER 6: INTIMACY . . . IN THE DESERT OF LONELINESS

[1]Augustine, *Confessions*, in *The Spiritual Formation Bible* (Grand Rapids, Mich.: Zondervan, 1999), p. 583.
[2]Craig Childs, *The Secret Knowledge of Water* (Seattle: Sasquatch, 2000), p. xiv.
[3]Gerhard E. Frost, *Journey of the Heart* (Minneapolis: Augsburg, 1995), p. 34.
[4]Julian of Norwich, *Showings*, in *Praying with Julian of Norwich*, ed. Gloria Durka (Winona, Minn.: Saint Mary's Press, 1989), p. 46.
[5]Ibid., p. 100.

CHAPTER 7: VICTORY . . . IN THE DESERT OF TRIALS

[1]Eugene Peterson, *A Long Obedience in the Same Direction* (Downers Grove, Ill.: InterVarsity Press, 2000), p. 116.
[2]A. W. Tozer, *The Pursuit of God* (Camp Hill, Penn.: Christian Publications, 1982), p. 16.

[3]Thomas Pierson, quoted in C. H. Spurgeon, *The Treasury of David* (MacLean, Va.: MacDonald Publishing, n.d.), 2:8.

[4]Amy Carmichael, "Toward Jerusalem," in *Learning of God, Readings from Amy Carmichael*, ed. Stuart Blanch and Brenda Blanch (Fort Washington, Penn.: Christian Literature Crusade, 1986), p. 32.

[5]Amy Carmichael, "If," in *You Are My Hiding Place*, ed. David Hazard (Minneapolis: Bethany House, 1991), pp. 34-35.

[6]Ibid., p. 125.

CHAPTER 8: THE SACRED . . . IN THE DESERT OF ROUTINES

[1]Victoria Brooks, *Ministering to God: The Reach of the Heart* (Cedar Rapids, Iowa: Arrow, 1996).

[2]Henri Nouwen, *Life of the Beloved* (New York: Crossroad, 1992), pp. 48-49.

[3]Ibid., p. 88.

CHAPTER 9: RESURRECTION . . . IN THE DESERT OF DEATH

[1]Dietrich Bonhoeffer, *Life Together* (New York: Harper & Brothers, 1954), p. 101.

[2]Dietrich Bonhoeffer, *Letters and Papers from Prison*, in Richard Foster, *Streams of Living Water* (San Francisco: HarperSanFrancisco, 1998), p. 81.

[3]Dietrich Bonhoeffer, *Life Together* (San Francisco: HarperSanFrancisco, 1993), p. 31.

EPILOGUE

[1]Craig Childs, *The Secret Knowledge of Water* (Seattle: Sasquatch, 2000), p. xi.

APPENDIX: JOURNALING THE JOURNEY

[1]These covenants are discussed in greater detail in Richard Foster's *Prayer: Finding the Heart's True Home* (San Francisco: HarperSanFrancisco, 1992), pp. 72-75.

[2]Ronald Klug, *How to Keep a Spiritual Journal* (Minneapolis: Augsburg, 1993), pp. 76-79.

[3]Jeanne Guyon, *Experiencing the Depth of Jesus Christ*, in *The Spiritual Formation Bible* (Grand Rapids, Mich.: Zondervan, 1999).

Marsha Crockett is available for speaking engagements.
If you would like to schedule Marsha at a conference or retreat,
contact her at <marshacrockett@hotmail.com> or write to

Marsha Crockett
c/o Canyon Creek Community Church
251 N. Roosevelt Avenue
Chandler, AZ 85226